thoughts +
affirmations for
on-ramping women
returning to work

WORDS
FOR
THE
JOURNEY

by Carol Camerino

CCMC, CTTCC, CCM, CBBSC
Back To Work Strategist & Resume Writer

Credentialed Career Manager
Certified Career Management Coach
Certified Tough Transitions Career Coach
Certified Brain Based Success Coach

Published by Sydney Hill Press, LLC

Author's Note and Disclaimer

The information contained in this book is meant as informative only and is presented with the understanding that the writer is not providing professional career services. The author assumes no responsibility for errors or omissions arising from use of the information herein. As there are many factors that impact employment and career success, the author provides this information to support jobseekers without any guarantee or assurance of employment or results. Readers are encouraged to engage the services of career services professionals for additional information and support.

Sydney Hill Press, LLC
New Jersey

Dedication

Words for the Journey would not have been possible without the women with whom I've had the pleasure of working. Their determination, grace and poise continue to take my breath away.

The world is a better place because of you, dear sisters. I'm so much better at my work thanks to your generosity of spirit. You pushed yourselves, trusted in yourselves and me, AND gave 110% effort to finding your on-ramps. **BRAVA!**

I dedicate my book to them as well as my family and dear friends — all of whom have been amazingly supportive and enthusiastic in their support of my work and this book.

Table of Contents

Introduction

Words For The Journey is a book of affirmations and intentions — plus a bit more — for women returning to work.

The path to writing this book has been circuitous. Actually, it hasn't been all that dissimilar to the journey traveled by on-rampers.

Initially, I thought I was writing a how-to book for women returning to work after a significant time away. As I mused and harangued, the idea for this book, the one you're now reading, kept popping into my head. I've learned the hard way that sometimes we just need to go with the creative flow, and so decided the how-to book will come later. With that, I rolled up my sleeves and began writing.

As you travel your on-ramping journey back to work and career, you may encounter detours, layovers, road construction and wrong turns. It is my sincere hope that this book serves as a trusted companion along the way; an important addition to your on-ramp atlas. May it provide that extra dose of inspiration, boost of confidence, oomph of motivation and more... at just the right times as you're traveling this new road.

Why a book especially for women returning to work?

My passion for helping women return to work is twofold.

First, I believe in the skills, traits and personal power that are curated and achieved through off-ramping or taking time off from career to care for family or to focus on non-work priorities. Honestly, I should say that I believe **wholeheartedly** and **passionately** in the skills, traits and personal power that women develop through off-ramping.

Truth is, off-ramped moms and women represent a largely untapped and skilled talent pool for employers and organizations. These skills, developed and honed outside of the traditional

ABOUT ON-RAMPS & OFF-RAMPS

Sylvia Ann Hewlett's book *Off-Ramps and On-Ramps* (Harvard Business School Press, 2007) is a rich resource on the phenomenon of women and nonlinear career paths.

As the CEO of the Center for Talent Innovation (formerly the Center for Work-Life Policy), Hewlett is at the forefront of the changing work-life landscape and leads employment policy making and policy changing research studies.

To learn more, visit www.talentinnovation. org.

workplace, are valuable to prospective employers. However, it is a necessary and difficult challenge to explain and translate these skills and achievements within the context of the traditional workplace.

While it may take some time for the hiring world to fully comprehend the value proposition of this amazing group, we can begin to pave the way by showing up at our best and being prepared to translate and bridge our skills and achievements. The route you travel as an on-ramping woman will surely see other footsteps walking along behind you. Those following journey women will be grateful for your trailblazing!

Next, I was a Stay At Home Mom (capitalization intentional!) for a few years and then worked part-time for many years. Probably like you, my time 'at home'[1] contributed greatly to the woman I see when I look in the mirror. I learned patience, project management, time management, conflict resolution, multi-tasking, the fine art of juggling multiple priorities...and much, much more. I fully understand that my professional skills and abilities have been immeasurably enhanced by my off-ramp time.

Despite the important skills learned during my time away from work, the transition back to the business world was a bit bumpier than I had anticipated. In retrospect, I realize there were some things I could have done to ease the transition a bit. And like hikers who mark the trails to ease the way for those following the journey, it's a privilege for me to share strategies and tips to help make the on-ramping journey smoother and easier for the next women embarking on their journeys.

Aren't there lots of books about returning to work?

Yes, there are. In fact, I've included some of my favorite books on careers and job searching in the last section of this book for your continued reading and learning. While some of these books include information specifically for women returning to work after off-ramping, there are very few that are designed for women who have been away from the work world for a significant period of time. Many career books for on-ramping women are written for those who have either been out of work for just a few years and/or those with advanced degrees from top tier schools who left work having already achieved significant career milestones.

Words For The Journey is for ALL women on-rampers... especially those who off-ramped from careers still in development and who, years later, look out at the career vista with emotions that include a sense of wonder and possibility as well as some trepidation and fear. As I wrote this book, I pictured the many women who left work 10, 15, 20 or more years ago and are now planning their returns. The roadway back can be challenging, and my goal is to provide a travel guide for these amazing and motivated women while they forge ahead and find their on-ramps back to work.

Three Parts

Words For The Journey has 3 parts. The first part includes background information about women and on-ramping (returning to paid employment) and affirmations/intentions (what they are and how they can help inspire and facilitate personal growth). The second part of the book is comprised of the affirmations and intentions. In addition to the affirmations and intentions, each page includes ideas, resources or actions to support you as you move forward. The final section, Part 3, is a resource list of some of my favorite on-ramping resources and websites along with some short articles from my blog.

PART 1

CHAPTER 1
YOU'RE ON YOUR WAY

Congratulations on opening your copy of **Words for the Journey**!

Whether you've purchased this for yourself, received it as a gift or picked up a copy at your library, the mere act of opening the cover signals the beginning of your next chapter … finding your on-ramp back to work. No matter how long it's been since you've last received a paycheck — 1 year or 20 — you're beginning an awesome journey towards achieving your career, financial and personal development goals.

If this leaves you breathless, there's a reason.

This is a time of amazing transformation. You're embarking on a sacred[2] journey. I've been witness to women stepping into their power, verbalizing dreams and wishes and supporting one another as sisters, friends, mothers and daughters. The inner confidence and radiance that grows from within once a woman acknowledges her potential and gifts is remarkable.

I daresay, it's one of the best anti-aging treatments available! There is a radiance and power that bloom within women as they tap into their inner gifts and strengths in a way that is very different from how they do so in their roles as wives, moms, sisters and daughters. This radiance begins as a flicker and, with time and attention, ignites to change how we feel and how others perceive us.

The Best Beauty Treatment Money CAN'T Buy

A while back, I ran into a woman who had participated in one of my 8-week job clubs. I didn't recognize her at first, but sensed she was familiar and that we had met before. I watched her for a few minutes, wracking my brain. As I ran through the list of how we might know one another (supermarket? soccer stands? volunteering?), I suddenly realized she had participated in one of my job clubs[3].

While there was a definite resemblance to the woman who actively and enthusiastically participated in the job club, this woman standing just a few feet away appeared more youthful and more energetic. In fact, she was positively radiant and glowing. I couldn't wait to get her attention and catch up!

She excitedly told me that she had found a job, was taking Zumba® classes regularly and felt better and younger than she had in years. I am not exaggerating in the least when I share that she looked AMAZING and telegraphed an air of enthusiasm, confidence and vitality. With a newfound understanding of her gifts and power, along with an expanded sense of possibilities, she was in bloom.

The process of reinvention — that is, getting in touch with yourself beyond your role as wife, daughter, mom and/or sister and embracing your life experience and increased wisdom, is an amazing life stage. Sure, it can feel unsettling as your self-definition is being re-configured and transformed. It's also richly empowering and rewarding.

Wondrous, even!

Its physical manifestation is a renewed twinkle in one's eye and a bounce in one's step. There is a youthful vitality that rolls onto the horizon and begins to add color and brightness to even everyday routines. It's a magic eraser that turns back the calendar and infuses excitement, hopefulness and an openness that positively scream youthfulness.

Try and find THAT at the beauty counter — at any price!

What Brought You To This Moment?

Returning to work after having off-ramped many years ago can bring a rush of emotions. In fact, one of the truths about on-ramping is that it can be a confusing time marked by periods of self-doubt and self-criticism alternating with feelings of hopefulness and anticipation.

The rush of emotions that can rule this stage are actually quite varied. As we consider the different — and highly personal and unique — reasons that women elect to look for their on-ramps back to work and career, this is not surprising.

For some women, returning to work at this particular time and stage of life has been part of the plan all along. Have you always known that you'd be returning to work at a future date? If so, you may have spent time thinking (possibly even dreaming) about what your new job or career might look like. Perhaps you've even been looking forward to this time of reinvention and getting back in touch with the 'career' you. Launching your self-discovery and career exploration campaign and subsequent job search, while stressful at times, may be seen as a wonderful new journey.

Sometimes, however, women find themselves looking for their on-ramps out of necessity. Rather than arriving at this stage happily and willingly, life circumstances have prevailed that make the need to return to work now, at this particular time, a priority.

Finding work, receiving a paycheck and linking into benefits may be a matter of economic survival. Unfortunately, there are myriad situations that can shake a family's financial foundation — illness, job loss and divorce to name just a few. If you're looking for your on-ramp because of an unexpected life event, this time may well feel scary and pressure-filled.

If you're grieving a change in your family status and lifestyle, please know you're not alone. This is a time and stage of life where leaning on others can buoy you through some rough patches. Reaching out for support[4] can provide a touchstone for your journey. This support, in the form of local nonprofit agencies, clergy, counselors, coaches, and mentors can help you to develop a new perspective and acquire necessary strategies for handling the stress and pressure.

So, whether you're returning to work by choice or necessity — or some permutation of reasons and causes, this is a time marked by uncertainty. And as in other times of uncertainty, you may wish someone would just tell you what to do or hand you the answer. Unfortunately, there is no grown up Magic 8 Ball, nor is there a person other than you that can provide you with your answers.

The paradox of learning to be comfortable with uncertainty will help you weather the seas of indecision and uncertainty. As you move forward, there will be times when you'll be faced with choices and must make a decision in order to move along. Of course, it's difficult to make a decision or selection without being able to peer ahead and see into the future. You might feel like a contestant on the game show Let's Make A Deal. Remember how they'd have to decide between what's behind curtain A and curtain B with only knowing a teensy bit of information? Their choice would land them either a prize...or the dreaded zonk.

I remember watching this show as a girl and feeling the anxiety and indecision right along with the contestants! How, I wondered, could they possibly make a choice when there were so many unanswered questions?!?!

Sometimes during your job search and career exploration, you'll be faced with a situation very much like what those contestants faced. You'll worry and harangue over making the right decision. And this uncertainty can make it challenging to take the next step forward towards your goals.

"Wouldn't it be helpful to have all of the answers before heading out on my on-ramping journey?" you might be thinking.

What About Having
The Answers Before I Start?

Uncertainty can be very tough.

Personally, I've never been very good at handling uncertainty. As a young girl, I remember being flummoxed by grownups who would say 'We'll see....' What exactly was there to see?! Just say 'yes' and let's move along, I'd think to myself.

As I got older, I grew to understand the wisdom of letting things ride a bit before making a decision or committing to something. However, patience and comfort with uncertainty are still not my strong suits. I understand how frustrating they can both be!

As someone looking for her on-ramp, you're going to be put in a position to make decisions about directions and choices without having all of the information. Sometimes you can wait to gather more information or clarity. The 'we'll see...' approach will make sense and serve you well. But sometimes you'll need to make a decision based upon only the information at hand, a hefty dose of faith and trust, and not much more. This latter approach flies in the face of how we've been taught to make decisions: gather all of the information, weigh options and then make a decision...right?

It's human nature to want to know where we're going, how we'll get there and when we'll arrive. Think about your last vacation. I'd venture to say that before you headed out of town, you'd already decided upon where you'd go. You probably also figured out your route, whether you'd be driving, training, busing or plane-ing and an approximate arrival day and time. Again...all done BEFORE actually starting the trip.

When you're looking for your on-ramp back to work, though, it's nearly impossible to plan the details in advance. It's that 'being comfortable with uncertainty' principle mentioned earlier. Personally, I think there's a yet-to-be-discovered muscle group that controls just how comfortable we are with uncertainty and not having all of the answers. And like other muscles, we can increase strength and endurance by pushing ourselves bit by bit.

Keep in mind, from the outset, that it's HIGHLY unlikely that you'll have all of the answers, insights and solutions you'll need from the very beginning. Here's what you need to remember... Despite the questions, the feeling unsure, and the not knowing all of the answers...

Go ahead and take the first step.

And the next.

And then the one after that.

Take one step at a time and you'll cover much ground.

"But what if I mess up...don't I need the answers before I begin?" you might be asking. The answer is a most emphatic **NO**.

You can't possibly have all of the answers regarding where you'll work, what you'll do, how you'll handle childcare for every possible scenario, and more at this point. As you move through your process, exploring possibilities, tapping into your wisdom and experiences, connecting with a network, and understanding financial truths, the options will begin to crystallize. It is from this point — a vantage point further down the road — that you'll be able to address these questions and find effective solutions.

Taking a step...and another step...and yet another step is a way to maintain forward momentum. And that forward momentum is so important. Without it, we can get mired in the weeds and lose sight of our destination.

Despite knowing that uncertainty is a normal part of the process, you may find that you'll become 'stuck' when focusing too much on details and issues that aren't essential to the task at hand. When you find yourself tangled in the weeds of minutiae, it might be that you're hyper-focused on the small stuff as a way to avoid the bigger, more important...and usually more difficult...stuff.

Where Will You Have Lunch in Santa Fe?

I know from first-hand experience that the weeds of minutia are a wonderful distraction from the big picture.

Here's an example of how it shows up. One day about 2 years ago, three friends and I gathered at my house for a day of writing. As we were brainstorming around our projects, we took turns at harnessing the collective creative energy in the room to get feedback on our respective projects. At the time, all of our writing projects were embryonic. We had outlines, notes, and pages written here and there. But suffice it to say that none of us had a book proposal or manuscript draft completed.

What were we spending most of our time talking about?

Not writing.

Not research.

Not organizing ideas, story ideas, and chapters.

No… those discussions would have made great sense, mind you. But they were not the focus of our discussions.

What were we spending time talking about?

Publishing options!

Yes, even though none of us had a book completed and each of us was in various stages of beginning with our writing and creating, we were focusing on the details and minutiae of publishing…getting an agent, submission strategies, book proposal development and even book promotion.

As someone who used to be (and sometimes still is) an over planner and over analyzer AND, as a result, a procrastinator par excellence, I recognized my good friend, Analysis Paralysis, lurking in the room. You see, our discussion surrounding publishing options was completely unnecessary at that stage of our projects. Spending time discussing and debating was not only a waste of time, it also served as a wonderful distraction from the actual work of writing.

It was then that a road trip analogy popped into my head. I shared it with the group by saying, "Worrying about this now is like us hopping in the car for a drive across the country and spending time talking about what we're having for lunch in Santa Fe 5 days from now instead of mapping out our driving route and figuring out where we'll stop and rest tonight!"

This 'lunch in Santa Fe' metaphor is one I've since used in job clubs and with clients. As you're on-ramping, you'll be tempted to fall into analysis paralysis and the need to have everything figured out before you move forward at all. You may also get hyper-focused on a component of your on-ramping plan at the expense of forward momentum. Unfortunately, these usually result in inertia and the inability to progress.

To help counteract this, I encourage job club participants, job search clients and you to take it one day and one step at a time. Just move forward every day, no matter how incremental it may seem. These steps combine to create an irresistible forward momentum that propels you forward.

CHAPTER 2

AFFIRMATIONS AND MINDFUL INTENTIONS

We're learning more and more about how the brain works. This new knowledge is fueling additional study into motivation and mindset. This new insight has implications into how we learn, push past negativity, achieve goals and develop a sense of well being and optimism. As someone who works with job seekers, this new insight informs my work as optimism and resilience are assets in the job search process. If you're interested in deepening your own understanding of this field, I encourage you to research and read more.

My interest is particularly focused on how to harness and channel our thoughts so they work for us rather than against us by undermining success or acting as internal subterfuge.

Maintaining a positive outlook and reframing our thoughts can impact mindset and channel positive energy in a way that supports us in working towards our goals. In fact, as I learn more about affirmations and mindful intentions, I'm reminded of Pygmalion. In the classic tale, Eliza is turned into a society lady because someone believes she can be transformed. But what if we turn this power inward and begin to send those messages to ourselves?

How do affirmations work?

Thoughts have power. Words have power.

Every day, we set our path through our thoughts and words.

Louise Hay, founder of Hay House publishing and best-selling author, explains that the universe takes its cues from us in regards to helping make what we believe a reality. In *You Can Heal Your Life* (Louise Hay, 1999, Hay House, Inc., Carlsbad, CA), she says, *"The universe totally supports us in every thought we choose to think and believe."*[5]

Pretty powerful, don't you agree?

Thrillingly powerful, actually.

Think about it. If you believe that you're not lucky or think that you're never going to find work you enjoy that provides you with financial security, the universe may well oblige. Likewise, if you believe that good things WILL come your way and that you WILL do work that provides financial security AND enables you to find personal fulfillment, the universe may also oblige. Which scenario is more appealing to you?

In the *Love Yourself, Heal Your Life Workbook* (Louise Hay, 1990, Hay House, Inc., Carlsbad, CA), Louise Hay quotes Dr. Bernie Siegel, a well-known author, physician and Yale professor in explaining why affirmations matter, "... affirmations are not a denial of the present, but a hope for the future. As you allow them to permeate your consciousness, they will become more and more believable until eventually they become real for you."[6]

By mindfully considering the **Words for the Journey** affirmations, you'll be allowing them to permeate your consciousness. They are seeds you are planting today. As you mull them over in your mind, glance at them throughout the day and re-write them on paper, you're tending the garden. In time, sprouts will appear and you'll begin to experience the power of positivity.

Here's an important point to remember, though. Yes, words have power. But affirmations and mindful intentions aren't magic. Simply repeating words without consideration, contemplation and even some action won't magically make things happen for you or change your reality. So stating "I'm going to make a million dollars this year" and then sitting back and waiting for it to appear is VERY unlikely to yield much by way of an enhanced portfolio.

For our purposes, let's focus on harnessing the power of positivity to support your reinvention and on-ramping journey. This is about tossing the self-defeating, negative perspectives and gloomy self-talk to the curb and replacing them with positive, productive and possibility-prone ones instead.

Whether you subscribe to the Law of Attraction or have noticed that we can support our internal calm and well being by monitoring what we see, think and spend time on, the bottom line is the same. If you focus on negative things, it sends a pall across our vision and we subconsciously look for proof of why things are so grim. If, however, you head out in the morning ready and open to see all that is good, you're more likely to notice the good such as the kind stranger opening a door for someone and the buttery, fresh smell of deliciousness as you walk into your local bakery. Ahhh...

So, consider how mindfully setting intentions and fertilizing them with affirmations and actions can serve to germinate the seeds of success and personal reinvention.

A while back, I wrote a post for my blog that compared Ruth Krauss' *The Carrot Seed* [7], a classic children's book, beautiful in its simplicity, to a job search. If you haven't read the book, I encourage you to get a copy. It's a pretty powerful tale about faith...and so much more. I'd like to share the blog post with you here:

JOB SEARCH WISDOM FROM A CLASSIC CHILDREN'S STORY

Ruth Kraus' *The Carrot Seed* tells the journey of a little boy and his gardening adventure. The boy plants a carrot seed and waits for the magic to happen. Despite some familial pessimism about whether the seed will actually develop into anything, the boy dutifully tends his garden; watering, weeding and watching. When there are no signs of growth, what does the boy do? Well, he keeps watering, weeding and watching. Eventually, a sprout appears and the boy is ultimately rewarded with a rather tasty-looking carrot! Ahh...success :-)

I loved sharing this book with my kids, and used it in my classroom when I taught preschool. It never failed to open discussions beyond the actual story. *The Carrot Seed* is about so much more than gardening or planting. It's about solidarity of purpose, resilience, delayed gratification, power of focus & intention, and faith.

These principles also happen to be integral to a successful journey back to work. As an on-ramper, you spend time writing and customizing resumes, creating cover letters, updating skills and knowledge, networking.... Like the boy in Krauss' classic story, you may not immediately see any evidence of progress. And family and friends may not provide you with the encouragement you desire.

But...stay the course. Pace yourself, maintain your stamina, and keep on keeping on. The boy in the story didn't plant the seed, water it once, and sit back waiting. He continued to tend his garden, even when he couldn't see results. And you'll continue to move forward with your job search strategies, gathering insights, networking, polishing skills, and possibly reaching out for assistance in the form of workshops, job clubs, or coaching, even when signs of progress are not visible.

You will eventually see results. And, with perseverance and patience, your garden will bloom, too.

CHAPTER 3

HOW AFFIRMATIONS WORK

The Red Purse

Can you relate to this? You've just bought a red purse. It was something you've wanted for months, and you stumbled upon a particularly adorable one that you couldn't resist buying and bringing home.

Now that you are the proud owner of said red purse, it seems everyone has jumped on your bandwagon! Everywhere you turn, you're seeing red handbags. School concert — red purses. Out to dinner — red purses. At the movies — more red purses.

Did you start a new trend?

Not likely, I'm afraid.

You see, the number of red purses roaming about your community and favorite spots hasn't increased. It's probably stayed relatively constant despite the fact you're seeing them everywhere.

What's going on then? Why exactly are you seeing red purses seemingly popping up everywhere?

While the number of red bags in your zip code hasn't changed significantly, something within your brain has. It's now on high alert to notice each and every red handbag that comes your way. It's received a red alert message (pun definitely intended!) to zero in on red purses because they've become a cranial 'item of interest' that is now simply irresistible and can no longer be ignored.

So, what exactly does a red purse have to do with affirmations?

Training Your Brain To Notice

The same process that allows your brain to notice something that hasn't been registering on your internal radar can work to our advantage when using affirmations. Affirmations, vision boards, goal setting...they're all kind of similar in that when done consistently and with focus, they put our brains on alert, too. But instead of looking for red purses, your gorgeous brain is seeking items that are in congruence with either the affirmation or goals.

In other words, your brain is working FOR you. It's going to notice ideas, thoughts and opportunities that can help you reach your goal. And with considering the affirmations, saying them, writing them, and keeping them front and center, they'll be more apparent to you. It's the red purse phenomenon...only better.

Isn't the brain an amazing and beautiful structure?

Boards of Possibility — Affirmations in Pictures

Vision boards, or Boards of Possibility, are a graphic representation of future paths and goals. I love vision boards and have used them myself and with groups over the years. In fact, creating 'Boards of Possibility' is an activity we do in my 8-week job clubs. It's a turning point for many participants and a confirmation for others who gain a clearer sense of where they're heading.

It's this clarity and insight that are important. Returning to work, reinvention, achieving….they all come from a dream or vision and become a goal.

We create vision boards as depictions of what we hope to bring into our lives. We then set goals to provide a target for us to strive for. In other words, vision boards are a pictorial reminder of dreams and wishes, and goals help us to set our path. Once goals are set, it's time to explore timelines, actions, and priorities. The loop is then closed when a roadmap (or action plan) for reaching and achieving these is created.

Board of Possibility How To

You can create a Board of Possibility alone or with a group. If you'd enjoy the synergy that comes from creating alongside others, invite some friends over for a creative and inspiring afternoon!

MATERIALS NEEDED
- Poster board or blank canvas
- Scissors
- Magazines (assorted, 3-5 per person)
- Markers
- Tape/Glue (Mod Podge if using canvas)

PROCESS

1. Flip through the magazines, tearing out any photos, words, illustrations, color combinations that speak to you. Set a time limit of 15-20 minutes. The point here is to not over think. Rather, just tear out whatever appeals to you.

2. When time is up, take a few minutes to review your selections, looking for themes and groupings. If you're doing this with a group, go around the room and ask about any surprises or findings.

3. Arrange the clippings on poster board and glue/tape down. How you arrange these is up to you. You can have things hanging off the page, overlapping, in neat sections...whatever strikes your fancy!

4. Add words and illustrations as you see fit using the markers.

5. Sign and date the vision board on the back.

6. If you're doing this in a group, have each person write a note about what she learned about each vision board creator and give to her as a gift. Spend time reading these aloud and discussing. It can be very powerful to hear how your ideas and pictures are reflected through the eyes of others!

Affirmations Vive La Difference!

Affirmations are a bit different from Vision Boards. They are a tool to use as a bridge between today and tomorrow's goal achievement. They facilitate us looking for the positive, the opportunity, the assistance.... the very items you've placed on your vision board.

Let's use a fitness analogy to describe how these tools work together.

If you wanted to get in better physical shape, your vision board would probably contain photos, sayings and emotions that capture the way you hope to look and feel when you've improved your health and fitness. Your goal in the process includes your specific weight, measurements and fitness levels (i.e., to run a 5K in under 40 minutes). The affirmations are the daily, weekly and monthly self—talks that keep you moving forward, that keep you focused and provide you with the support to keep going. Without them, you might lose steam, get distracted, begin to focus on difficulties and challenges instead of keeping a positive outlook.

One Affirmation, Many Meanings

Have you ever watched a movie with friends only to discover afterwards that you each have completely different thoughts and ideas about the film? Each person watched the movie through her own eyes, sifting through the emotions, motivations and landscape of the film. You sat as a group to watch the film, but experienced the film as individuals. Were you even watching the same movie, you might wonder to yourself.

Affirmations are like that, too. Have a few people read the same passage and you're bound to get different interpretations.

While the words of an affirmation are clear to all who read them, the meaning can be, and often is, highly personal and even possibly situational. We translate the words through our own unique lens of experiences, emotions, hopes and fears. Our gorgeous and mystical brains help us to distill what it is we need out of the particular collection of alphabet soup within our very own context of time and place.

Not only can each person interpret an affirmation according to her experience, re-reading the same affirmation a few weeks or months from now can lead to a completely different yet important understanding. Again, from the vantage point of where you are, who you've met and what's transpired, you will interpret the words as they suit your new circumstances. New thoughts and feelings may be present and different actions and strategies manifested as you consider the words within the context of a new place in your journey.

Time and Consideration

The power behind affirmations doesn't come from reading the words once and then moving on. Rather, the benefit comes from spending time thinking about them and considering how they relate to what's happening at present. Affirmations require time to ponder and time to consider. Ask yourself, "What do these words mean to ME?" and "How can I apply the meaning behind the words to my present and future situations?" Figure out what works for you and incorporate that into your plan. For me, focusing on an affirmation or intention for a period of at least several days helps me to internalize it. Throughout this time, the real message becomes apparent and gets downloaded on a more meaningful and deeper level.

Using affirmations takes time; time to implement a daily practice and time to begin to see results. Changes won't happen overnight. But setting aside time in the morning and evening to mindfully consider an affirmation, to write out the words on paper, to say them aloud, to post them around your house...whatever works for you, is a way to infuse the power of affirmations into your reinvention and on-ramping process.

CHAPTER 4
AFFIRMATIONS AS A PRACTICE

It's ironic....during a stage in life that is often marked by uncertainty, fear and self-doubt, the road to success requires emotions and thoughts on the completely opposite side of the spectrum.

Use the affirmations and intentions here as a beginning to support your on-ramping from a perspective of hope, positivity and optimism so you can tap into your inner confidence, spark and wisdom. Let them start a new way of thinking about the future and approaching your own goals and destiny. May they help you tap into your power and greatness in a new way that you've yet to experience.

The world of work...the world in its entirety, for that matter, needs you. Who knows what your impact will be?

Perhaps you'll help turn a business around. Maybe you'll inspire coworkers. Or you just might set an amazing example for your kids and grandkids. But if you don't take the first step, and then the next one and the following one, none of us will ever know what new greatness you are meant to achieve.

Words for the Journey includes over 50 affirmations that can be used daily or weekly. Consider using an affirmation for several days at a minimum to really absorb the idea and intention.

Personally, I like to keep the words front and center for several days to a week or more. That's what seems to work best for me. However, there is no 'perfect' way to develop a practice around affirmations and positive intentions. Try a few different approaches until you find the strategy that fits your learning style and personality best.

Here are some ideas to get you started:

■ Start an affirmation journal where you write about the statement and how it came into play throughout the day.

■ Copy the affirmation onto pretty paper or into a notebook and post it in a prominent place as a reminder (bathroom mirror? refrigerator?).

- Make the affirmation your screen saver.

- Make the affirmation your smartphone wallpaper.

- Clip the affirmation to your calendar or appointment book so you're glancing at it throughout your day.

- Put the affirmation into a frame on your nightstand or desk.

- Read the affirmation silently several times a day.

- Create an action plan around the affirmation, using the information on each affirmation page as an idea starter.

- If you use an e-calendar, set the affirmation as an appointment twice a day or so, so you're sent a reminder.

- Start an affirmations discussion group with some friends and supporters. Meet monthly or every two weeks, focusing on 2-4 affirmations, discussing how they've impacted each person's actions, activities and outcomes. Share ideas, thoughts and dreams as you cheer one another on! Every so often, dedicate a meeting to writing your own affirmations.

When you've completed the **Words for the Journey** affirmations, simply begin again. You can either start back at the first affirmation or randomly select one each day. Different thoughts and feelings will be evoked and different actions and strategies manifested as you consider the words within the context of a new place in your journey.

I give you permission to copy the affirmations onto index cards in order to re-use them easily. It might be fun to randomly pick one affirmation from the pile, trusting that you've selected THE perfect one for the upcoming week!

If you'd like a printable file of the affirmations, simply email me a copy of your receipt and I'll happily email one to you[8]. I respectfully request that you not share this with others as it's my gift especially for you.

May these **Words for the Journey** support you as you embark on this amazing journey back to the world of work. You will weather the bumps and detours elegantly as you reflect upon the messages contained in these pages. If I can be of any assistance, please email me at Carol@LookingForTheOnRamp.com.

The world of work awaits. Today is your day to start your journey!

PART 2
Affirmations

I am generous in spirit and graciously allow others to help and support me on my reinvention journey.

Thought

We often resist accepting offers of help, thinking that it's a self-centered or selfish act to receive without giving in return.

In reality, graciously accepting and receiving offers of assistance can be one of the most generous things we can do — for others. Rest assured, your turn to be the giver will come. May that gesture be met with the gracious acceptance that you now practice.

Action

Say 'Yes, thank you!' to the next offer of assistance you receive and recognize that it can be one of the most generous actions of your week.

I tackle challenges and setbacks systematically and methodically, focusing on solutions rather than history or blame.

Thought

When things don't go as planned or when we're in the midst of worry, fear likes to take over. And fear's close friend, blame, is usually not far behind. Unfortunately, both fear and blame serve as roadblocks to solutions and fixes.

Instead, focus on creating an action plan that moves you from today to tomorrow, next week and next month, with each day containing an incremental step towards solution or resolution. Break down strategies into specific steps and actions, setting reasonable timelines.

Action

Grab a large piece of paper and do a 'brain dump' around a particular problem or challenge. Write down every thought, feeling, idea, hunch...anything and everything that comes to mind. Review what you've captured and begin to create a plan by grouping items into categories.

I practice exemplary self-care {eating well, exercising regularly and getting appropriate rest} in order to radiate my inner power.

Thought

Like flight attendants remind us, we must place an oxygen mask on ourselves first in order to be of service to others. Be aware of how often you put the needs of others before the needs and priorities that are integral to your well-being, happiness and success.

Is there a 'false choice' that's being made?

Must you sacrifice your well-being to really meet the needs of others? Or might this actually undermine your care and concern for others in the long run as you degrade your ability to help by depleting your own well? You can attend to the needs of your significant others (spouse, kids, friends) from a stance of strength and power once you've honored and attended to your own.

Read

The Art of Extreme Self-Care by Cheryl Richardson

Listen

Gentle With Myself by Karen Drucker (available on iTunes)

I am attuned to the lessons that today's challenges are meant to teach me so that I may move closer to achieving my goals.

Thought

It's not easy to mine the difficult terrain of disappointment and upset for what are often the gems of wisdom. But knowledge really IS power, and gaining this kind of insight is priceless.

Action

Stop and ask yourself...

"What is the lesson here that I need to learn or the insight I need to gain in order to move past this roadblock or challenge?"

"How will this new insight impact me as I move onward and upward?"

"What will my process look like from this point forward?"

I believe this is my time to shine, flourish and nourish.

Thought

Consider the potential and possibilities that are awaiting you.

It IS your time!!

Dwell in the constellation of possibilities and dare to consider what could become your new reality.

Action

Create a "Board of Possibilities" that contains your hopes and dreams for the you of tomorrow. Let your imagination soar; there are no limits. Block off a couple of hours and create your very own vision board!

Supplies: poster board, markers, tape/glue, old magazines, scissors (detailed instructions on page 13).

...display your completed Board of Possibilities in a place of your choosing where you'll glance at it regularly and be reminded of what you're striving towards.

I take care to honor boundaries with friends and family so as to be fully present for ME.

Thought

The process of reinvention and returning to work IS a job. It requires focused time and energy. Set appropriate boundaries so that you have the time and energy to create and execute a successful return to work strategy.

Action

Track the times that you put your own wishes, tasks and responsibilities aside. Consider how these impact and impede your progress. Select one day a week that is sacrosanct – you cannot add any activities or events for or with others. This one day is all about you – your goals, your objectives, your action steps. Beyond the essential daily chores associated with your role as caregiver, you're not to add anything else. These blocks of time will come to be sources of accomplishment and inspiration that nourish you along your journey and propel you forward.

If an entire day doesn't work for your temperament or responsibilities, how about two mornings? Two afternoons? One evening?

If your neighbor calls and asks you to go for a walk on this day, the answer is 'Thanks for thinking of me, but I'm booked."

If your child's school calls asking for a chaperone for the field trip, the answer is, "Oh, I would LOVE to ordinarily, but I've got another commitment on my calendar for that day."

It's empowering to claim your space and honor your boundaries.

I walk proudly and confidently with a smile on my face and a deep sense of self-knowing regarding my power and ability.

Thought

You are your most important cheerleader and advocate!!! Practice projecting your inner confidence and light to the world so that your true gifts can be acknowledged and appreciated.

Have you ever caught sight of yourself in your laptop's reflection or accidentally switched your phone camera lens to reflect back at you?

I have.

I almost didn't recognize the grouchy, grumbly, pinched face reflected back at me. It's a real 'in your face' and humbling reminder of how others might be seeing us. The experience has impacted my self-awareness. I want a countenance that radiates kindness, love and openness – and I'm much more conscious of my default facial expression as a result.

Action

Catch yourself in the mirror or window reflection as you're going about your day.

Are you smiling?

Do you appear happy?

Set reminders several times a day to smile and unscowl. Your 'smile muscles' connect to your brain. Before you know it, you'll be feeling AND looking happy.

I WILL land the perfect job for me as I am today — and will learn all I can as I strive to move towards achieving my long-term goals.

Thought

Your next job need not define you. Rather, it can be a step closer to your long-term goal.

Economic realities may dictate that you consider taking a job that provides you with a paycheck for now, for today. The reinvention and new career will follow a bit further down the road, when financial constraints are resolved or minimized.*

Here's an important point: whatever position you take as your on-ramp job, be the best {fill in the blank} there is, impressing co-workers and supervisors with your ability to learn quickly, work hard and contribute to the team.

In the meantime, you will create a corps of supporters and advocates that will serve you well in future career steps.

Action

Research opportunities for adding to your skillset. Select one that fits your schedule and budget and boldly take the step to move forward towards your goal. Set a timeline with action steps and select an accountability partner to serve as your cheerleader and supporter.

*Research scholarships and low/no cost training programs that can make retraining and going back to school very affordable. Start your research by calling your local women's center and unemployment office.

I set myself up for success through impeccable time management.

Thought

Time is a commodity that cannot be saved, stopped or created. It simply is...

Time moves forward on its own, whether we want it to or not. Be meticulous with how you allocate this precious resource, blocking off time for important activities and tasks and allowing time to BREATHE. If you find yourself in a familiar battle against time, be ruthless with your calendar and frankly assess your scheduling and planning.

Time, or lack of time management more specifically, is one of the largest hurdles for job seekers and on-rampers. Are you scrambling to find time to launch and execute your job search? Are you not allowing the appropriate time to be successful? Finding a job IS a job, and it takes dedicated time and resources.

There really is no substitution for putting in the time and utilizing solid time management strategies.

Read

Getting Things Done – Stress Free Productivity
by David Allen.

Action

Block off time in your calendar at the beginning of each month for your job search. Consider these blocks of time to be immovable!

I say NO when it suits me.

Thought

To share a quote by Anne Lamott, one of my favorite writers, "'No' is a complete sentence."

No explanations or reasons needed.

Enough said.

"NO."

Action

Just say "No."

I plan time in my day to just BE as I honor the quiet and solitude, recognizing its ability to water the seeds of creativity and possibility.

Thought

Sure, finding a job and the process of reinvention are the result of multitudinous steps and actions. Busy, busy, busy will you be!

BUT.... wise is the woman who takes time to sit in the stillness and contemplate direction, possibility and purpose for it is in this stillness that insights are brought forth from within.

Action

Sit. And be still.

...That's it.

Just LISTEN; to nothing.

No music.

No TV.

Shhhhh.....

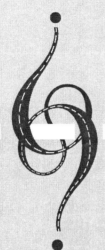

I marvel at and celebrate where I've been, where I am and where I'm heading!

Thought

Look at you!!

You are pretty amazing – juggling all you do, caring for your friends and family, and sharing all that is uniquely you to the world.

As you think of your journey to date, what will you celebrate?

Personally, it's never a party or real celebration to me unless the music is playing. Music has the power to transport us to another time and place and to rev things up from gloom to ZOOM!

How about cranking up the tunes and celebrating?! Below are a few of my favs to get your playlist and celebration started.

Action

Create your very own 'Celebrate ME!' playlist.

Listen

Happy by Pharrell Williams
Brave by Sarah Bareilles
This One's For The Girls by Martina McBride
Today Is Your Day by Shania Twain
Unwritten by Natasha Bedingfield
Firework by Katy Perry
Who Says You Can't Go Home by Bon Jovi and Jennifer Nettles
Don't You Know You're Beautiful by Kelli Pickler
I Am Light by India Arie

I recognize fear and doubt as necessary partners in my journey as they are often hallmarks of important transitions and change.

Thought

The voices of fear and doubt, and possibly their very negative and potentially destructive cousins, self-criticism and hyper-criticalism, often come to roost during periods of change and transition.

Action

Welcome them, recognize why they're here, give them just a cursory listen, and then send them on their way!

Listen

If you could use some additional strategies for keeping those voices in check, listen to the audiobook version of **Taming Your Gremlin** by Rick Carson.

I am organized with my time, workspace and possessions so I may concentrate on the actions necessary to launch my reinvention.

Thought

Is your space cluttered and disorganized?

Do you have to send out a search party when you need paper, writing utensils, printer ink, or stamps?

Nothing drains energy and brings momentum to a screeching halt like clutter and disarray. With disorganization and clutter as the norm, you can feel like your on-ramp is paved with quicksand.

Action

Consider setting aside time to address this head on. Whether you devote an hour a day for several days (or weeks) or decide to invest in a professional organizer, clearing your space can be like adding rocket fuel to your engine!

Read

It's All Too Much by Peter Walsh
Move your Stuff, Change Your Life by Karen Rauch Carter

I cultivate a YES mindset that opens doors to new opportunities, friendships and experiences.

Thought

Are you a 'no it all'?

Do you think of all of the reasons why something WON'T work instead of all the reasons why it WILL?

As a mom, I began a slide on the slippery slope from 'Sure, why not?' to 'No!'. Before I knew it, I became 'all no-ing'. I caught myself saying 'no' almost as soon as my son or daughter would begin their requests. Borne out of worry and concern, this default of 'no' can stifle growth and independence — in our children and us.

With 'no' as an almost automatic response, we cut ourselves off from fun, spontaneity and opportunity. Think of how that impacts reinvention, on-ramping...and life in general!

I have a dear, dear friend (she knows who she is!!) who has taught me the wondrous power of 'why not' as opposed to 'why.' It's one of the most transformative phrases I've ever uttered.

Action

The next time you're about to say 'no' to something (interview invitation, job offer, lunch date, event invitation...), think twice. Switch your mindset to a default of YES and watch what happens!

Read
Age of Miracles — Embracing the New Midlife by Marianne Williamson

I honor and appreciate the opportunity to practice and hone my skills.

Thought

Increasing and updating one's skills makes you a competitive job seeker and contributes greatly to your job search success.

Have you taken the time to assess which of your skills need to be updated and enhanced in order to be competitive in today's job market? Consider what these may be for you and your job target, and then roll up your sleeves and start practicing and learning.

Action

There are myriad ways to attain new skills – from those that are free all the way to university degree programs that require a significant investment.

Evaluate the options and develop an action plan for increasing your marketability in your chosen career path.

Once you commit to a program, course or self-study plan, appreciate and honor the opportunity rather than feeling grumbly about it. Remind yourself how incredibly wonderful it is to learn, to invest in yourself (via time, money or both) and to watch the wonder that is you expanding and growing in knowledge, skills and insight.

You rock!!

I have all of the help and wisdom I need within arm's reach and can find solutions and assistance with ease.

Thought

An amazingly insightful (and talented!) business coach, Sierra Sullivan*, shared this idea: all of the help we need is already here, within arm's reach, but for the asking.

That's a pretty powerful thought, don't you think?

As she shared this at one of her fantastic women's retreats, we marveled at how true this was. Right in the space of the retreat, connections were forged, plans were made, and outreach was begun.

This sentiment applies to you and your job search, too.

Who is just off in the wings, ready to support and assist you?

Action

Create a resource list of your 'go to' people - who they are, their areas of expertise and contact information.

Reach out to the people on your list and ask if they'd be willing to serve as accountability partners, networking contacts, technical advisors and cheerleaders as you step boldly into this new stage and phase.

Extend yourself by serving as a resource for those on your list, too.

*Sierra Sullivan is cofounder of Life Stylized, a personal empowerment and small business consultancy based in Saratoga Springs, NY. To learn more, visit http://lifestylized.com/.

I learn new skills quickly and embrace innovation, technology and social media as opportunities for enhanced effectiveness.

Thought

Simply put, solid computer and technology skills are essential in our 21st century job market.

Tech proficiency is now an assumed competency. Companies are usually not willing to train employees in the basics. As such, you may need to spend time becoming comfortable in this brave new work world that revolves around virtual communication, relationships and creativity.

Whether you're going to be working in retail, sales, nonprofit, business, management, admin...anywhere, you need to know how to navigate technology.

Action

Create your own plan for moving your computer skills and comfort with technology up a few notches!

If self-study fits your schedule and budget, consider visiting your local library and checking out some of the 'Idiot's Guides' or 'Dummies' books focused on Microsoft Office, Mac, LinkedIn, Networking and Computers. Despite the snarky titles, these tend to be well-organized and easy to follow.

If you have basic proficiency in computers and technology already and want to add to your skills, check out Lynda.com. It's an online training source that covers basics as well as complex and expert-level skills. For a modest monthly investment, you can access 2,200 courses at present, with more being added!

Also consider community adult school offerings as a low-cost option. In addition to reasonable fees, this is also a resource for people who prefer a classroom setting and enjoy the accountability of being expected to show up for class prepared and ready to go.

I proudly and enthusiastically step forward with the knowledge that every step — no matter how small — brings me closer to my goals.

Thought

Lao Tzu, philosopher and author of the Tao Te Ching, is often quoted as having said, "A journey of a thousand miles must begin with a single step."

So wise. So profound.

Why is it that we all too often focus only on the celebration of the thousandth mile, though, and not the milestones along the journey?

As you move forward, how can you honor and celebrate your progress?

Action

Create your own special celebration — TODAY.

It doesn't have to be elaborate or expensive... perhaps you're going to crack open the novel you've been reading - right now — in the middle of the day {GASP} or treat yourself to a manicure.

The point is to celebrate the steps!

It's about the progress, not perfection.

I am wise, wonderful and worthy of career success.

Thought

Yes! You are!

Action

Say these words to yourself throughout the day. Bring the joy and power of this sentiment home with a playlist that celebrates the power of women like us.

Listen

Beautiful by Carole King

Do It Anyway by Martina McBride

I Am Woman by Helen Reddy

Natural Woman versions by Aretha Franklin and Carole King — both are amazing!

In France They Kiss On Main Street by Joni Mitchell (I'm a huge Joni fan and the chorus is so uplifting!)

I stretch myself beyond my comfort zone as I know it builds confidence muscles that will serve me well.

Thought

The comfort zone...the comfortable, easy, safe and well-worn path, how we so love thee.

While comfort zones are so, well, COMFORTABLE...they can also be a bit stifling to the old personal growth arena.

Comfort zones are to your career and life what lane bumpers are at a bowling alley. If you've ever gone bowling with children, you may have used bumpers. They are long contraptions that actually prevent bowling balls from going into the gutters. Bowling with bumpers means there will be no gutter balls...and the chance of hitting pins is exponentially increased.

The only problem is that to really learn the game, the bumpers are removed and bowlers eventually must learn how to propel the ball down the lane and hit pins using their own skill — and not depend upon the assistance of the bumpers.

Where in life or work are you relying on bumpers? Where might it serve you to push beyond your comfort zone?

Action

Think of something you've been putting off because it's just a bit scary or a bit intimidating and plop it proudly and loudly on your to do list.

Are you missing out on seeing movies you're longing to see because you can't find someone to go with? Do it! Go to the movies by yourself one afternoon {note: this is a fabulously empowering thing to do).

Do you walk through the yarn aisle at your local craft store and think to yourself how you wish you could knit? Buy the supplies and a 'how to' book and tackle it!

Do you love singing and wish you could capture the fun and joy of singing with a group? Research your area to find a local choir or chorus and show up. Look for one that's open to new members and, if it makes it easier for you, find one that doesn't hold auditions.

Is your job search stalled because there is one particular skill that you don't have as of yet...and it's showing up on job postings time and time again? Learn it! Teach yourself, sign up for a class or buy a book and start down the path to mastery.

I recognize serendipity as grace in action and readily accept the gifts and opportunities that come my way.

Thought

By recognizing serendipity as more than mere coincidence, you will be more attuned to the opportunities brought right to your doorstep — literally.

There really are no coincidences...

Have you ever been stuck in a quandary when the solution seems to mysteriously and fantastically drop from the sky?

It might be in the form of something like this: You realize that you need to be in two places at the same time next Thursday as both kids need to be picked up at exactly 4pm — but from opposite sides of town.

If only you could clone yourself, you lament! Then the phone interrupts your fretting. It's another mom asking if she can pick up Johnny from the after school club and bring him home for you as she was hoping to pick up the book you'd said she could borrow.

Problem solved!!

Serendipity, or happy accidents, comes in many forms... from networking connections, to smiles from strangers at just the perfect time, to blasts of insight at a much-needed moment.

Action

Be open. Be aware. Be thankful.

I get closer and closer to my employment goal each and every day.

Thought

It's easy to lose sight of incremental progress when our eyes on trained on the outcome!

But every day you're learning, exploring, considering and moving closer to achieving the goals you've claimed for yourself.

Action

Track your actions and progresses by writing them down daily in your on-ramp journal (a cute/stylish notebook you've dedicated to your return to work). At the end of the day, make two entries: one will be a celebration of what you've accomplished and the second will include items for future tackling.

I mine the jewels of my life experience to enrich my job search and provide insight into the gifts I bring forth to my future employer.

Thought

What you've done and where you've been have brought you to this point, to today.

There is no denying that you've gathered much in your journey to date. New skills, new attitudes, new strengths and new ideas are just a few examples.

Do you know how much you have to offer employers?

I often hear women express concern that they feel like they don't have marketable or transferrable skills for today's job market. While some of these job seekers may need to brush up on technical skills, the life skills gleaned during their time away from work can be valuable contributions to their overall candidacy.

Action

Spend time brainstorming the transferable skills you've mastered since you last worked. To get you started, here is a sampling of a few skills many women can add to their lists:

- multi-tasking
- budgeting
- time management
- organization
- project management
- conflict management

I welcome uncertainty in order to be open to opportunities and possibilities as my journey unfolds.

Thought

That unsettling feeling in the pit of your stomach when faced with uncertainty can quickly lead you to the state of 'getting stuck.'

In the book *The Worry Cure*, Robert Leahy, Ph. D., explains that one of the reasons for this is that people begin to interpret uncertainty with negative outcomes. However, he quickly points out that uncertainty is a state of neutrality, neither positive nor negative.

Imagine that!!

Read

The Worry Cure — Seven Steps to Stop Worry From Stopping You by Robert Leahy, Ph.D.

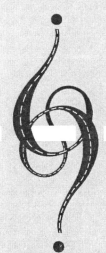

I approach my job search with enthusiasm and excitement as I become reacquainted with my work/professional self.

Thought

Remember her? That girl who went off to work each morning ready to tackle the day?

Guess what? She's still there. She's just waiting to step forward!

Recently, I spoke with a woman in a job club who had just begun a new assignment in an office setting after having been away for a while. When we spoke, I sensed a whole new energy. Her voice was bubbly, and though we were talking by phone, I could picture the lovely smile and sparkle in her eye.

This positive mojo came about because she said 'yes' to an opportunity.

And saying yes to this has ushered in a renewed sense of hope and energy. In fact, she mentioned how she's picked up her craft work again and is so looking forward to each day. Wow!

Action

Get back in touch with what you enjoyed most about your past job(s) as a way to tap in to possible career pathways for your reinvention.

Consider working with a coach or linking into career services offered in your community. Interest inventories can provide a starting point for exploring possible career paths.

How might the energy around your job search change if you approached tasks with 'Today, I get to…" instead of 'Today, I have to….'.

Radiating positive energy and enthusiasm can be the differentiator that results in a job offer.

I acknowledge closed doors as harbingers of better options and new pathways.

Thought

Alexander Graham Bell said, "Sometimes we stare so long at a door that is closing that we see too late the one that is open."

While there have been many iterations of this saying, they all boil down to the same sentiment: lamenting what is no more or what might have been can blind you to the array of possibilities that are now within reach.

Action

Consider what doors may have closed for you, either in the past or at present.

Think about how this might just be the 'perfect' problem. Perhaps it forces you to move outside of your comfort zone. Maybe it means you need to change gears, something you've been putting off...

Which new door is opening and beckoning you to step through?

I am energized by the prospect of returning to work and exploring my next chapter.

Thought

Change can be energizing...or draining.

Choose to view the start of your new chapter as exciting and wonderful to create a delicious and juicy momentum that will propel you forward. A whole new world awaits!

Action

What new approach, idea or strategy can you tackle today?

Adding change in small ways can support changes in bigger ways.

How about learning a new recipe, trying a new hairstyle or even changing your perfume?

Step out of the 'but that's the way I always do it' paradigm and embrace something new as you support your reinvention and add zing to the process.

I have a wonderful and encouraging network willing and able to support my return to work.

Thought

Over the years, you've met lots of amazing people — through work, through friends, through family and through volunteering.

Many of these people would be happy to reconnect — and may serve as fantastic networking connections.

Action

Give your network a boost by reaching out to those you know via Facebook, LinkedIn and Twitter.

Think of friends, family members, neighbors, classmates, former colleagues and bosses.

Expand your circle by researching to find a local chapter of a professional networking group to connect with, too.

Reach out to your alumni association and professional organizations to add to this list.

Reconnect and catch up with friends or colleagues you haven't seen in a while over coffee.

I am prepared for my
interview and look forward
to the opportunity to share
why I am the solution
they've been looking for.

Thought

Newsflash: Interviewers and employers are in need of what you have to offer.

Think about it: you're being interviewed because they have a vacancy they need to fill AND something about YOU has prompted them to INVITE YOU to discuss how you might be just the person they've been looking for!

How wonderful it is that you're getting the opportunity to pitch YOU!

Action

Do your homework and prepare for the interview. This is not the time to draw upon your improvisation skills. To ace the interview, research the company, the job and the industry. Be sure you know your resume inside and out. Be prepared with some compelling CAR (Challenge-Action-Result) stories.

Take a look at Harvard Professor Amy Cuddy's engaging, inspiring and relevant online TEDtalk on power posing. You'll be gifted with some ideas for upping your confidence level in interviews.

I mindfully craft cover letters and emails, sending them on their way with positive thoughts of success.

Thought

Clients are sometimes disappointed to learn that the one-size-fits-all cover letter is no longer a strategy that works. There simply is no one cover letter that applicants can use across the board. Rather, targeted and customized letters are the recommended approach.

Action

Adopt several cover letter templates that you can refer to as you craft compelling cover letters. Do research so you understand the company culture and values. Use this information to enhance and inform your writing.

In addition to writing compelling and well-crafted cover letters, how about harnessing the power of intention by thinking positive thoughts as you hit 'send' or stand at the mailbox? Envision the recipient positively noting how your qualifications and skills and match so perfectly those listed in the job posting. Imagine how you'll respond when you receive a phone call or email inviting you to move forward in the selection process.

Read

Job Search Magic by Susan Whitcomb

I am attuned to my gifts and profoundly aware that I will make a difference.

Thought

Women returning to work after a significant time away bring a level of insight, compassion and work ethic that the world needs. Tune in to how your life experiences have prepared you to make a difference — for your employer and/or coworkers, colleagues and clients.

Action

Think about how the you of today might approach some of the challenges your earlier self faced. Whether it was a challenging customer, a difficult colleague or a tyrannical supervisor, the wiser and savvier you of today would approach these situations from a different vantage point.

Consider how this vantage point perfectly positions you for today's workplace. Be prepared to share this value-add to prospective employers.

I manage my money effectively and understand that investing in my personal finance skills is essential.

Thought

It's 10 pm — do you know where your money is?

Okay, that's an attempt at some humor...but to make a point. How are the dollars and cents being spent? Can you account for them? Or do you open your wallet and think, "Where did that money go??"

Having our finances in order helps to assess salary offers. Doing the work in this area provides much-needed data that shapes on-ramping, including knowing how much money you need to meet monthly obligations.

Action

Speaking with a financial planner or your banker can pay off in increased financial acumen and the development of a long-term plan. Some planners and banks even offer workshops especially for women and finance.

Research upcoming financial seminars in your community.

Visit www.suzeorman.com and www.jeanchatzky.com for informative articles, resources and upcoming programs.

Read

Smart Women Finish Rich by David Bach
Does This Make My Assets Look Fat by Susan Hirshman

I am mindful of the power of chance meetings so take care to set the stage for making an amazing first impression by showing up polished and presentable.

Thought

I still remember the time 15 years ago when I went to my local supermarket very early on a Saturday morning wearing what could have passed for bona fide pajamas...makeup-less, in a state of barely combed hair, and wearing my outdated 80s-style HUGE glasses.

As I stood in the bread aisle, I gasped when I realized that the dad of one of my son's friends was right next to me. I was hoping the floor would open up so I could drop through and hide.

As he turned and made eye contact with me, I was ready to sputter something about how I had run out NEVER expecting to see ANYONE. I then realized my excuses were unnecessary. As we made eye contact, there wasn't even a glimmer of recognition. I looked so unlike my usual self, that he had no idea that he was standing inches away from someone he saw and spoke with often. Perhaps he was being chivalrous and was simply saving me from embarrassment. Either way...Yikes!

While certainly relieved that my cover wasn't blown that day in the bread aisle, I learned an important lesson. You never know who you might meet — it could have been my boss, a colleague, a mentor, or even Jon Bon Jovi (insert name of your celebrity crush here). The takeaway for me — and for you — is to leave the house looking presentable. You don't have to be magazine photo-shoot-ready all of the time. But you do need to look like you've taken some care and pride in your appearance.

Action

Build in the extra 15 minutes (really, that's all it takes) to add a bit of polish to look pulled together before walking out the door. My 'never leave home without it' includes mascara, tinted moisturizer, lipstick, and no sweats – ever. Sorry, but I subscribe to the Seinfeld philosophy: wearing sweatpants in public sends the message that you've given up – at least in so much as you've decided it's not worth the minimal effort and energy to go the extra millimeter to kick things to the next level.

Read

Style Statement by Danielle LaPorte and Carrie McCarthy

MORE magazine by Meredith Publishing

The Small Things Blog (www.thesmallthingsblog.com) by Kate Bryan

I read inspiration and insight written by some of today's most interesting voices in order to deepen my understanding and form my own views.

Thought

Thanks to the internet, we have access to modern day prophets and visionaries as well as contemporary genius and wisdom of the ages. And it's all right at our fingertips!

I believe you are what you eat. I also believe that we are shaped by the information we invite into our lives...whether it is via TV, the big screen, music lyrics or the written word. Why not infuse positivity, possibility and wisdom into your world through your reading?

Following is a sampling of some of my favorites. They're my virtual 'go to' group that I turn to in order to push myself, expand my thinking and increase my well of inspiration. Some of what I've read has formed the woman, writer, coach, wife, mom and friend I see when I look in the mirror!

Marianne Williamson	Louise Hay
Wayne Dyer	Anna Quindlen
Mastin Kipp	Carolyn Myss
Gabrielle Bernstein	Maya Angelou
Danielle LaPorte	Anne Lamott
Mary Oliver	Maria Shriver
Deepak Chopra	

Action

Curate your very own list of inspirers to whom you'll turn
for wisdom and encouragement. Who are the writers and
thinkers that speak to your heart?

I take time to exercise and eat well, nourishing my physical body in order to robustly navigate the on-ramping roadway.

Thought

Feeling good is one of the best anti-agers there is. As on-rampers, it's important to telegraph an air of vitality and youthfulness, of high energy and enthusiasm. One way to do this is to adopt a nutrition and exercise plan that supports your well-being.

Action

Schedule a visit with your physician to give you the once over. During times of stress (and reinvention can be stressful!!), taking care of ourselves can fall to the wayside. Seeing your doctor to address any health concerns and to create a well-balanced lifestyle plan can be more youth preserving and longer lasting than an expensive face cream.

Check out healthy lifestyle, cooking and fitness resources online and at your local library.

I remember that rainbows appear after the rain.

Thought

On-ramping can be a bumpy journey at times. There will be rain on your parade...putting a damper on your enthusiasm and energy. What can you do to usher in the lovely rainbows that arrive as the storm rolls out to sea? At times like these, I find it helpful to borrow some positive music mojo until my own levels are back to their optimal levels.

Action

Who knew?

Turns out there is a biological reason that certain songs make you happy and peppy! Music can actually alter brain wave frequency. Read *Your Playlist Can Change Your Life* by Galina Midlin, Joseph Cardillo and Don DuRousseau for tips on creating a playlist that will kick start happy, optimistic, and energizing brainwaves into high gear. The book even provides song suggestions.

What songs will be on your rainbow-producing, rain-rain-go-away playlist?

READ:

Your Playlist Can Change Your Life by Galina Midlin, Joseph Cardillo and Don DuRousseau

I nurture and encourage relationships with friends.

Thought

Connecting with friends is balm for the soul.

Sharing, laughing, connecting — it's all so wonderfully supportive and nurturing!

Action

Throw a dinner party — an old-fashioned potluck where everyone brings a dish. The point isn't to impress everyone with your Cordon Bleu-like culinary expertise. The REAL reason for the evening is to tap into the collective energy that gathering with friends can bring.

Personally, I'm a fan of the workweek dinner party (as opposed to a Friday or Saturday night) as it just feels SO sophisticated and cosmopolitan. But pick any day of the week that works for you. Make it a somewhat regular event, too. Monthly? Quarterly? You decide...

Don't be surprised if you start a new trend!!

I remember in the deepest and most knowing part of myself, that I have options and choices — always.

Thought

Yes, we don't always have control over turns of events or situations.

But we do have control over our reactions.

Tap into your personal power by remembering that you do, indeed, have options and choices.

Action

CHOOSE your reaction.

CHOOSE your direction.

CHOOSE how you'll spend your time.

CHOOSE with whom you'll share thoughts, desires, goals and dreams.

Remind yourself...you have options and choices.

I tap into the wisdom and support of my very own team of cheerleaders.

Thought

So often, we feel like we need to go it alone. However, this is a time for reaching out. It needn't be a crowd of people...but think of at least one or two special, positive people that can serve as a sounding board, cheerleader, proofreader, and shoulder to lean on. Ask them if they'll stand with you during this important time.

Action

Who is on your team?

Which friends, family members, and neighbors can you enlist for your cheering section?

Make a list and reach out to the special people you've identified to let them know you're hoping you can count on them for their support.

I appreciate being present and mindful, focusing on rituals and tasks throughout the day.

Thought

How often do you multi-task your day away — barging through the day, grabbing lunch on the go, coffee on the go, making phone calls while grocery shopping....

Are these really time savers?

How different might your days be if you carved out 10 minutes for a real cup of coffee...in a ceramic cup or mug, enjoyed sitting comfortably in one place?

How about taking 5 minutes to make the phone call and actually focus 100% on the conversation?

It's very Zen...and very nurturing.

Give it a try.

PS: Have you heard? Multi-tasking is very over-rated!

Action

Vow to uni-task!

Start by concentrating on a small task — just one — in its entirety, excluding all distractions (tame that monkey mind*!!). If it's your morning coffee or tea, actually sit at your table and feel the warmth of the cup, inhale the lovely aroma, take a sip and savor the taste.

Be in the now and luxuriate in the ritual.

*monkey mind is a meditation reference to the wandering, jumping and distracting thoughts that can pop into our heads at random, disrupting our focus and concentration.

My to do list and calendar support my vision and goals.

Thought

How focused and intentional are you about your reinvention and return to work? Paying lip service to it and acting on it can be two very different things. One way to assess whether the rubber really is meeting the road is to take a look at your calendar and to do lists.

If your schedule is filled with everything BUT career-related items, it might be time for a reset.

Action

Assess your activities over the last several weeks and for the 3-4 upcoming ones.

How many of these are items dedicated to moving you forward?

This exercise can be somewhat sobering in an 'in-your-face, show me what you really, really want' kind of way.

If many (or preferably, most) of your activities and commitments are aligned with your return to work goal, well done you!

If your analysis points towards room for improvement, there's no time like the present. What items need to come off your calendar in order to make room? And what activities, commitments and 'to dos' need to become integrated into how you spend your time and energy?

I have a dedicated space from which to launch my return to work so that my attention and focus are rightfully supported.

Thought

On-ramping requires researching, writing, phoning, applying...and more! Do you have a 'control central' from which to operate? That is, a dedicated, organized and inspiring space to support your efforts? If your materials and thinking are spread throughout your house, you can feel disjointed and as if your job search is a second thought.

Action

Set aside an area of your house for your very own "On-Ramping Resource Center". It can be a Rubbermaid bin with files, labels, pens and paper or it can be a dedicated home office. The non-negotiable is that it is off limits to everyone except you. Keep it neat and organized so that you pick up seamlessly from where you left off and can continue on.

I keep up to date in my industry in order to fully understand emerging trends and issues.

Thought

Reading is fundamental to career success.

You want to be seen as someone who is current regarding trends, ideas and news in your field and expertise. You'll use the information you learn from reading and researching in cover letters, networking settings and interviews.

Action

Set aside time each week to read about your work, your industry and trends so that you're seen as someone 'in the game.'

Sources of information include online news sites, professional journals, blogs of key thought leaders, books, professional association websites and whitepapers.

I connect with helpers and advocates who are uniquely positioned to support my on-ramping journey.

Thought

What organizations and resources are available to help you navigate the roadway back to work?

Area nonprofits? Job Clubs? Career Coaches? Resume Writers?

Your alumni career placement office? Your state unemployment office?

Action:

Pick up the phone and make some phone calls to begin to uncover the help that's available right in your backyard!

Prepared to be stunned — in a good way — by how many people are ready and willing to support you — for the asking!

I project my best self by wearing clothing that fits, reflects my style, and is in good condition even when I'm staying at home as I know the power of feeling good about myself.

Thought

As someone who does a fair amount of work at home, I know all too well the temptation to lounge around in pjs, sweats or yoga pants. I also know how differently the day can go when I start it off in a quasi-polished and stylish outfit — even if I don't have any in-person meetings or appointments. My energy increases, confidence heads north, and productivity multiplies.

I may not be meeting with anyone or going anywhere, but feeling polished and put together makes me feel good. And feeling good is pretty darn powerful when you're looking for your on-ramp or launching a new career!

My friend Janet Cargill, author of **Look Damn Good — At Your Age, With Your Body and On Your Budget** and image consultant extraordinaire, talks about the energy and power that comes from throwing open your closet door and knowing that everything in there fits, looks amazing on you, and reflects who you are.

Her book details a 10-piece wardrobe that translates into many, many outfits. While I confess to having more than 10 items in my closet, I'm happy to say that I have significantly fewer items today, thanks to reading Janet's book, learning her style tips and knowing how to shop efficiently and effectively. This pared down closet has made mornings less stressful. I also feel more confident stepping out in clothes that I feel good in!

Action

Review your closet and keep only what you love AND only what looks amazing on you. Donate or give away items that are still usable, as someone else will surely enjoy them.

Read

Look Damn Good – At Your Age, With Your Body and On Your Budget by Janet Cargill

Lessons From Madame Chic by Jennifer Scott
(Check out her blog, *The Daily Connoisseur*, too, for a peek into infusing French chic and that certain 'je ne sais qois' into your life.)

I trust in the ebb and flow of daily life — not overly stressing when inevitable challenges crop up as I understand that grace will usher in opportunity.

Thought

Life surely has its ups and downs.

And so, too, does the on-ramping journey!

Face the inevitable bumps in the road, detours and u turns with aplomb — not allowing yourself to be thrown by them. Sure, there will be disappointments and frustrations. As one door closes, know that another one — one that may well be best – will open.

Action

The next time things don't go as planned, make the decision to allow yourself only a set amount of time to lament and harangue over the aforementioned bumps, detours and u turns.

When this time is over, say aloud to yourself "OK, that's enough of that! Time to switch gears!!"

I make time for exercise and movement as feeling strong and energized adds to my confidence and vitality.

Thought

Getting a move on physically works wonders for your overall well-being!

Despite knowing this, many of us don't make time for it. One reason is the sense that it's costly to join a gym or yoga studio.

But working out doesn't have to cost a lot. No need to join a fancy-shmancy gym. Take advantage of what's around you for free!

Action

You might power walk in the mall. Better yet, take it to the streets...and trails and paths. Put on comfy clothes and 'sensible' shoes and start walking.

Consider NOT being plugged in, too. Walking outside, whether in a bustling city or a foresty wood, not only gets the old heart pumping, but it also transports us to a kind of meditative state where the most amazing and powerful ideas and insights bubble up into our consciousness.

Carry your phone for safety reasons if needed...but no chatting, checking email, or texting.

I recognize that maintaining a big picture vision beyond tomorrow supports my dreams and goals.

Thought

Where do you see yourself in 1 year? 3 years? 5 years?

Without a sense of direction, you can get VERY off track. Keeping a long-term vision in mind as you move through the weeks and months can help you to stay on track.

Taking the time and energy to consider a big picture, long-term view of our careers is powerful. It supports a focus on making things happen instead of letting things happen.

Action

Regularly set aside time to consider the questions of 'Where do I see myself in 1 year? 3 years? 5 years?' to support you in achieving your goals.

Block out time to review where you are and where you're heading by placing appointments with yourself right on your calendar. Take stock of your progress, note any course corrections that may be needed, and even consider if your long-term goals have changed.

Some questions you might ask yourself as you audit your progress might include...

How is my progress as compared to my initial plan?

What course corrections do I need to make?

What have I learned about myself? My goals? My strategies?

When I look back on this time, what is it I want to be able to say about how I handled and managed things?

What activities/accomplishments are sources of pride?

Remember, you can also tap into your support team to help you keep your vision in your sight.

I appreciate and honor my friendships, drawing upon the life experiences, wisdom and generosity of these sisters for support and encouragement.

Thought

Lucy and Ethel. Laverne and Shirley. Tina Fey and Amy Poehler. Friends do, indeed, make the world go 'round.

When life gets crazy, we can sometimes feel disconnected to the very people who recharge our energy and cheer us on.

How powerful a force close friendship is to help us surmount challenges, deflect negativity and spur us to action!

Action

Grab your phone and call one of your close friends just to let her know how much you appreciate her and that you so value her friendship. Add one or two reasons why she's important to you and then sign off with something like 'I'm so profoundly happy to have you in my inner circle!'

I look for opportunities to be of service as I make new contacts and expand my network.

Thought

Old school networking, the model where people operate as if there is a race for shaking the most hands and amassing the biggest stack of business cards while also barely concealing that they're scanning the room for someone more important is SO yesterday.

Today's savvy networkers look for opportunities to be of service — sharing information, providing referrals and making introductions.

Action

Before you attend your next networking event, set an intention for what you'd like to achieve.

Mine is usually to find just 2 or 3 new people to connect with and to leave with dates to meet for coffee or lunch. In addition to your intention, look for an opportunity to help someone...perhaps recommending a book he/she might like, suggesting a website as a resource, or making an introduction to someone helpful.

Within 24 hours, reach out to the connections you've made and share a resource or set up a time to talk further over coffee.

I honor the playful part of me, making time for fun and laughter — both with friends and when alone.

Thought

When is the last time you changed into your play clothes and let loose?

In our results-driven world with its maniacal focus on practicality, production and performance, VIP (Very Important Play) time gets short shrift.

A few years ago, I stumbled across a book in a hotel lobby that was transformational for me. The title was Permission To Play. In fact, I've since decided that it was left there especially for me to find as it was EXACTLY what I needed to read. I left it on the lobby table at the end of my vacation for the next lady to find, and quickly ordered a copy of my very own. I now keep it on the coffee table in my reading room to flip through and refer to easily.

Action

Plan fun time into your calendar. Whether it's doing something fun (hula hooping, crafting, biking, watching a comedy...whatever is fun for YOU), plan to work it into life in regular doses.

Visit www.meetup.com to check out fun events in your area that are appealing to you. Book talks, hiking groups, choruses, board game aficionados...the possibilities are truly endless!

Read

Permission To Play — Taking Time To Renew Your Smile by Jill Long Sourcebooks, Inc., May 2003

PART 3

On-Ramp
Miscellany

BLOG POSTS

Excerpts from the Looking for the On-Ramp blog (www.lookingfortheonramp. blogspot.com) — short articles I've written about returning to work, job searching and careers.

The term 'Comeback Moms', used in a few of the following posts, refers to women who left the world of paid employment for a time following a maternity/family leave and are presently seeking a return. Please replace the term with 'on-ramper' if that is more appropriate for your situation.

In Spite Of –
A Poem for Job Seekers

In spite of...

In spite of...

In spite of...

It's dark.

The path is unclear; you're unsure of where to start.

No matter that this day wasn't what you had hoped it would be.

The stars will shine tonight, their light in the velvet night sky like the spray of soap bubbles, ready to clear the remnants away and leave a fresh new canvas.

What a gift these stars are, reminders that their glimmer means you get to start anew.

Yes, tomorrow IS a new day.

"Hello stars!" you might say tonight. "Work your magic and usher in my next chance, my new opportunity."

When you wake, the stars will be gone. Their sparkle, magic and power now dissolved into the new blank slate that is today.

In spite of...

Time Wrangling

One of the most common challenges faced by jobseekers has to do with wrangling time; that is, how to focus energy and efforts on a regular basis to move one's job search campaign onward and upward.

There is simply no substitution for rolling up your sleeves and tackling your job search. With the timeline for finding jobs being fairly long, a day spent diverted from the job search can mean an added number of weeks of life without a paycheck.

How will you create your days and weeks to reflect your priority of finding a job?

That's not a rhetorical question. It's a bonafide, serious, lay it all on the table kind of question. Finding a job IS a job. Trying to squeeze in time for your job search is short-changing your campaign.

What is it that's keeping you from moving forward? If you're finding that you aren't able to spend time on your job search, it might be time to assess and reflect. Here are some questions to consider and discuss:

1. **Direction:** Where are you heading? What kinds of jobs are you targeting? What type of workplace are you interested in? Sometimes not having clarity around your goal can leave you feeling unsure of next steps. Procrastination (in the sneaky form of allowing other events and commitments derail your progress) can result.

2. **Future and Possibilities:** What will success look like? What are the payoffs of landing this job? Starting with the end in mind and peering out to the landscape of sweet success can be very motivating.

3. **Getting Unstuck:** Is your runway cleared for takeoff? If your space is cluttered, it might be also zapping your energy and enthusiasm. What can you do to create a space that nurtures and supports your job search?

4. **Power Scheduling:** Are you organizing your days to take advantage of your best times? If you're a morning person, what will it take to tweak things so that your are able to hit the ground running during your peak performance time?

Once you've explored some of these questions, it's now time for some R&R (renovation and radical new plans). Assess your calendar, paying particular attention to non job search-related commitments. Which of these can be pushed aside or rescheduled for 8 weeks from now?

Go ahead and make way for your job search in a manner that supports your forward momentum. You'll gain traction and make progress towards your goal that will infuse the rest of your journey!

The Modern World of Work

I've been hearing a catchy, clever tune on XM Coffeehouse while driving around town. Modern World by David Wilcox describes how 'this ain't the modern world that I remember.' He's referring to the 60s and 70s rendition of the future. You remember, the one with flying cars, space colonies, smell-o-vision, and Jetson-esque homes and workspaces.

Today's workplace has not been completely Jetson-ized. But if you off-ramped 10 or more years ago, you may be surprised by the workplace a la 2009. Understanding how it has changed provides you with a framework to envision yourself thriving and succeeding as your new on-ramped self. It can also give you important insight for talking about your skills and strengths in interviews and will give you a heads up as to what skills you'll need to polish and/or master.

Here is a brief comparison of what the corporate work world was like when I off-ramped in the early 90s and on-ramped in 2006:

THEN

- The company I worked for (a major corporation) wasn't on the internet!! Businesses still weren't sure about this newfangled e-world. What we did have was a very unfriendly and clunky intranet, with monitors that weighed 50 pounds and took up a big chunk of one's desk!

- If someone read an interesting article in a professional journal that he/she wanted to share with colleagues, a routing slip was attached, and the magazine was passed from cubicle to cubicle, with each person checking off as he/she read it.

- Files, busting at their seams, filled people's in boxes. Managing the growing mounds of paper documentation was a constant struggle.

- The phone rang constantly.

- Everyone did their work in the office. Project not finished? That meant a mandatory stay at the office as there was no ability to work from home on a laptop.

- Meetings were held face-to-face in conference rooms and offices.

- Everyone wore suits.

NOW

- E-mail is everything! Colleagues a cubicle or office away send e-mails all day — interesting articles, updates on client requests, feedback on reports, checking whether you brought lunch or want to order out, etc.

- The phone doesn't ring very much. Client communication, prospective client communication, and communication with friends and family happen online the majority of the time during the workday.

- Microsoft Office rules the work world. I had fancied myself as fairly computer savvy when I on-ramped. The first day on the job I was asked to edit a fairly lengthy PowerPoint, replete with fancy graphics and links. I adeptly corrected typos, spelling and syntax — with a pen on the printed copy of the report. How embarrassed I was when I realized I was supposed to do it online! I felt SO old-fashioned — barely a step away from asking where the typewriter was!! After somehow muddling through the electronic version, I invested in a bunch of how-to books and practiced at home to get my skills up to speed. It became a personal badge of honor on those rare occasions when I could point out a shortcut to one of my younger, and way more e-savvy, colleagues.

- Meetings often happen virtually. Instead of traveling to meetings, they happen right on everyone's computer. Thanks to meeting software, trainings, client presentations, and proposal meetings can happen without the expense and time drain of everyone being in one location.

- Suits are worn rarely. Big client presentation? Definitely a suit day. Every other day, however, smart business casual is appropriate. Great slacks, blouses, sweaters, and accessories can definitely get you through many work situations.

- Laptops make work portable. My company allowed for work to be done at home — a policy that provided flexibility to meet important deadlines without the need for extended hours at the office. I appreciated the ability to work from home when necessary. If a snowstorm made roads treacherous, I could still put in some hours at home, keep on deadline, and not have to deal with a white-knuckle drive.

WHAT HASN'T CHANGED

Your life experience, patience, compassion, and smarts all work together to make you a wonderful asset to the world of work. I admit to being fairly intimidated by my highly intelligent and driven younger colleagues initially. It didn't take long, though, for me to realize that I most definitely had a lot to offer. I happily acted as their sounding board and helped them, as they helped me, too.

You can make a great comeback. It is nothing short of thrilling to imagine the impact you can make!

Moms & Tots Groups — Round 2

Remember Moms and Tots groups? These playgroups provided many women —
including me — with a treasured support of like-minded women who became
woven into the tapestry of their lives.

I was so very lucky to have Kathy, Tracy, Jean, Lisa, Mary, Diana, and Justine;
all whom lived within sugar-borrowing proximity. We met weekly, presumably
for the kids. However, I know that a huge part of our playgroup was for the
moms. We threw baby showers, sang happy birthdays, baby-sat, collectively
wringed hands over fevers, shared child-rearing challenges (remember the
terrible — er, I mean — terrific twos?), and celebrated each other's successes.
Those wondrous years as a young mom were made even more magical thanks
to them.

What power and strength these groups provided! As we transition to a new
stage now, one where we're on-ramping, finding our way back to jobs and
careers, we can channel this same support and enthusiasm! Stay tuned for
posts on starting a Moms and Jobs group, what these groups can do for moms
re-entering the workforce, and tapping into the inherent power of women
supporting and inspiring one another.

Silence The Critics

Who are you to write this book? Who cares what you have to say? No one is going to read it! How ridiculous you're going to look.

These are a sampling of the voices that have been speaking to me lately. Who are these people? They are the very voice of my self-doubt and criticism. And I am so un-inviting them to my book party!

Some background: I resigned from a great job in corporate communications about 18 months ago to pursue my passion — writing. Since then, I've been doing freelance work while also working on my book, *Looking for the On-Ramp: A Guide for Returning to Work.* As I get deeper and deeper into the book...and closer and closer to making my dream a reality...the thoughts above have been whispering into my ear.

Anne Lamott, one of my all-time favorite writers, describes the audience of voices that sit with her as she writes. "They are the voices of anxiety, judgment, doom, guilt....there may be a Nurse Ratched....." she explains.*

While it doesn't help to stifle the voices much, it does take some of the wind out of their sails. I realize this self-flagellation is all a part of the process, part of the human condition. And it certainly helps to know I'm not alone.

When I began my comeback to the business world, I remember a similar sense of self-doubt and fear. *"Excel?!? I haven't used Excel for anything beyond creating a roster as a homeroom mom,"* I thought as I figured out how to create a spreadsheet. *"Mail merge? No one said I needed to know that,"* I lamented as a wonderful colleague patiently sat with me — again — to show me how. "I am going to completely destroy the company's database," I feared as I walked myself through the query steps carefully.

Each of these voices seemed intent on shaking my confidence and sending me packing. However, I continued to will them into silence and worked on 'sharpening the saw,' a Steven Covey phrase that perfectly describes the importance of continual skill building and enhancement. Eventually, I became irritated enough with them and more comfortable with my abilities that they packed it in.

Comeback Moms have our own unwelcome whisperers who are keen to point out all sorts of things like your age, how long it's been since you've worked for pay, how hard it's going to be to get your resume together, how expensive it will be to go back to school, or how you're going to need a completely new wardrobe and hairstyle. In other words, these voices will try and shake your confidence and break you.

DO NOT LISTEN TO THEM!

Instead, carry onward and upward. Tell them to get lost, that you don't have time for their foolishness, that you're too busy to LISTEN: to their nonsense, tell them to SCRAM! Then, take one step at a time closer to staging your comeback. Each small step gets you a bit closer to your goal. And each step makes the voices a bit harder to hear.

*Anne LaMott, **Bird by Bird: Some Instructions on Writing and Life**
 (Anchor, September 1995)

Learn The New Lingo and
You'll Be The Bees Knees, 23 Skiddoo!

Slang: language peculiar to a particular group
(http://www.merriamwebster.com/)

23 skidoo and bee's knees were popular phrases from the 1920s. Can't you just picture parents rolling their eyes as the younger generations bandied these about? In our lifetimes, we've heard popular phrases come and go, incorporating them into our own lexicon as necessary and appropriate.

The world of work, regardless of your discipline, has its own set of lingo that changes over time. Virtually every sector of the employment market has new buzzwords and it's essential to make sure you're up to date on the current terminology and concepts that are popular in your field today.

So how do you go about getting the scoop on the new phrases you need to know? There are a bunch of strategies you can try.

Read Job Postings/Classifieds
Employers will often include acronyms or industry-specific terminology in their help wanted ads. Take note of those that you don't recognize and do a bit of research to expand your knowledge.

Informational Interviews
The value of informational interviewing extends way beyond learning about new buzzwords (an upcoming post will cover the reasons why you should consider informational interviews). While you are talking with a professional in your desired field, don't be shy about asking him or her to define terms. Make sure it's okay for you to take notes, too, and write down phrases or concepts you want to learn more about.

Internet Sources
Professional groups, industry organizations, and general websites are all possible places to look for additional information. Type a phrase or term into your search engine and start your research.

Professional Journals and Organizations
These often offer the latest trends and information in a given field. And reading posts and replies on message boards can provide great insight.

As you become more knowledgeable about your field's slang and buzzwords, you'll begin to develop a comfort level with authentically and knowledgeably using these in professional conversations. You may also find that you've discovered an area or concept in which you'll want to enhance your knowledge level or skill.

Um...How Long Is This Going To Take?

How long is this going to take? Exactly when will I land that job?

That, ladies, is the million-dollar question. And the answer is a Confucius-like "it will take as long as it takes."

You see, each woman's journey to the on-ramp and a job offer is so very unique and personal. A few lucky ones may merely need a dusting off of a resume, a quick tune-up of key interviewing skills, and a few new network updates to be off and running. For most of us, there is probably a bit more prep work and foundation building that need to be done to set the stage most effectively. But — no matter where you fall along the continuum, the steps you take will ultimately get you to your destination in good time.

Let's celebrate one another's successes....but without putting pressure on ourselves. Comparing your progress, or lack thereof, to the successes of others is like comparing apples to oranges. As with cooking, some dishes can be made quickly and easily while others take more care and simmering. The end results can be equally delicious!!

If you realize that your skills need updating, you are much better served by putting in the time now to upgrade or refresh them prior to your actual search phase as time spent now will pay dividends in your marketability as well as your confidence. As you support your friends in their job searches, you'll start hearing about upcoming interviews and job offers. Not to worry. You'll get there. After you get yourself in tip-top job search shape.

Look at your ultimate goal and create daily, weekly and monthly to dos that get you closer to finding your new place in the world of work. You can methodically and regularly tackle these. And how great will it be to cross them off one by one as you execute?!?!

The Secret You Shouldn't Keep

Who knows that you're looking for the career on-ramp and planning to re-enter the world of work? If you've decided to keep mum until you've accepted an offer, you're short-changing yourself.

An important strategy for job hunting in this brave, new world is NETWORKING. In other words, it's not always what you know...but who you know. If you don't let everyone know you're interested in going back to work, your job search will be a bit like trying to run a marathon in pumps. You may cross the finish line, but it's going to take longer.

Remember the Faberge Organics shampoo commercial from the 70s? The one where I'll tell two friends, and they'll tell two friends, and so on, and so on, and so on? That's what will happen with you and looking for a job.

By getting the word out that you are actively looking for a job, you will exponentially expand your network and increase your chances of landing a job.

So...who are you going to tell today?

Savvy Sobriquets

Momma4, tennismom1, and *gemini1968* seemed like great choices for your email handle.

But now that you're on-ramping, a mom returning to work, email names like these can land your resume and cover email in the spam or delete folders of the HR gatekeeper faster than a coach passenger trying to use the first class lavatory gets turned back at the curtain!

There is a pretty easy solution for getting a more professional sounding email. Create a new account with one of the free email service providers such as Gmail, yahoo, and Hotmail.

Check out http://email.about.com/od/awards/ss/The_Best_In_Email_2010_The_ Reader_s_Choice_Awards.htm *(click on Top 17 free email accounts article)* for descriptions of some of the popular options that are available.

When you create your new account, you'll be asked for your new username or email ID. Think about something professional, something that will be easy to identify you as, well, you. Consider using a combination of your name, something like jane.Doe, j.doe, doe.j, or doe.jane.

Having a professional email name increases your chance for success on several levels. Plus, it's a quick and easy to do that gets you closer to returning to work!

The Truth About Stay At Home Moms

Show me a picture of a stay at home mom and I'll say, "Check her odometer!!" The phrase, you see, is a complete oxymoron.

Not one woman I know who has 'stayed home,' really did. While we may have decided to off-ramp from career paths, many of us applied our business and project management skills to new venues. For moms who 'stayed home,' we accomplished lots of things: served on boards of directors of non profits, volunteered as officers of PTOs and PTAs, consulted part-time, volunteered in ministry work, used project management skills in logistical and financial planning for our homes...the list truly is endless!

How do I know about this? Because I was there in the trenches alongside you! I've seen how hard you work and how smart you are. I know what you have to offer to the world of work. Your work ethic is unparalleled, your ability to multi-task...well, let's just say you are one of the originators of the movement, and your teamwork skills are about as good as they get. In other words, YOU ROCK!

So, as you begin to create your resume and plan for going back to work, consider all that you've been doing 'at home.' We may have some teaching to do, helping companies and organizations understand how our achievements 'at home' translate into valuable workplace skills. But once we begin to show them what we've got, they'll be clamoring for other comeback moms to join their ranks!

Online Applications — The Agony!

Question

I'm looking to return to work. I've noticed that some companies have online applications. Do I need to fill these out, or can I just mail my resume and cover letter to their HR department? These online forms take so much time...UGH!!

Answer

This is a question that someone recently asked in one of my workshops. As a mom returning to the workforce, you're probably going to be visiting a variety of job sites and company websites. Often, there will be an online application of some sort that needs to be submitted.

Yes, I agree — these can take a significant amount of time and the frustration factor is sizable!!

You'll want to follow the company's procedures for applicants, though. While online applications are sometimes cumbersome, unwieldy, and time consuming, circumventing the official procedures can result in your resume getting tossed. Once you've done what is required, you can always send a well-done cover letter and resume via snail mail or email, referring to your online application. One major caveat...ensure that you are submitting your information to a reputable and bona fide employer before proceeding (perform appropriate due diligence and online research).

Tip for on-ramping

To make online applications a bit easier, create a reference sheet with commonly requested information already detailed (past jobs, responsibilities, dates, degrees, certificates, references, etc.). This way, all you'll need to do is refer to the sheet for much of the application. No need to keep recreating the wheel!

Stand Out In The Crowd —
How To Get HR's Attention

FACT
Some HR people receive dozens, maybe even hundreds, of resumes for job openings.

This begs the question of how to make yourself stand out in the crowd. It goes without saying that your resume needs to be in tiptop shape. But the truth is, at least some of the resumes that HR reviews in response to a vacancy will look as great as yours...and possibly even better.

So how exactly can you gain an upper hand at the beginning of the hiring process? I recently heard of an applicant who differentiated herself by going a bit above and beyond, and very nicely allowed her resume to stand out. How'd she do it? She sent along a reference letter that detailed her accomplishments and successes along with what made her a great employee.

One of the reasons this worked in securing her an all-important interview slot is that the letter took a bit of the guess factor out of the equation. The hiring person had actual documentation that she has accomplished all that her resume claims. And a letter of recommendation expands upon gifts and talents beyond what is put on a standard resume.

Put yourself in the place of a hiring pro faced with the prospect of screening dozens of resumes for one job. Let's say you ended up with 15 potential candidates who possessed the skill set you are looking for. How would you pare the list to a reasonable number to interview? Chances are, if the resume with the reference letter were among the 15, it would end up in the 'Yes' interview pile.

An Anti Aging Treatment For Your Resume

A great resume is like an investment wardrobe piece — classic and timeless. It doesn't scream an era or look out of style.

If you created your on-ramp/back to work resume using the same writing tips from back in the day, chances are your resume is out of style. If so, your resume may be ready for an anti-aging facial of sorts.

Here are 2 resume renewal treatments that can give your resume an updated look for a 21st century job search:

1. Be Objective About Your Objective
We all learned that objectives should talk about what we are looking for... advancement potential, room to grow, yada, yada, yada. Today, it's no longer "all about me." Organizations are looking for what you can do for THEM, not how they can help YOU. Use the old objective space to highlight what you bring to the table. Use keywords for your target market AND the job posting.

2. One Size Does NOT Fit All
Customizing resumes is essential. A generic resume that tries to promote your skills and abilities for any and all potential jobs just doesn't work. Tweak your resume to match what the prospective employer is looking for. I help my clients create a master resume for each of their target areas, and then teach them how to make slight changes depending upon a job posting or company profile. This way, they're not starting over each time. Rather, they're making small changes that take their resume from good to GREAT!

Timing Is Everything

It's been said that finding a job IS a job. And whoever said it first was right!

Deciding to return to work is a huge decision for many women. But it's really just the beginning of an exciting and wonderful new journey. Finding the on-ramp requires that you carve out designated job readiness and job search time.

What?!?

You may be thinking about how busy you are already and wondering how to cram more to dos into your day. You're not alone. It is a challenge at first...but it's essential to finding a job as well as great practice for getting your family ready for your return to work and the changes this inevitably brings to the family.

If you've made the decision to return to work, take a look at your calendar and begin protecting blocks of time that you will dedicate to the process. The amount of time you'll need depends on a variety of factors and is unique to your situation. I suggest starting out slowly...perhaps you'll dedicate just an hour or two weekly to start, using the time to read some great articles or conducting online research.

Once you begin to put some structure around your process, you can add time and gain additional momentum.

It's all very exciting...wonderful... and a bit unnerving, perhaps.... But I'm here to help. Visit my website for information about my services and upcoming programs.

Music To Job Search By

Today I heard a song that made me stop and take a listen:

Shania Twain, a mom making an amazing comeback and finding her on-ramp back to her music career, has written what could very well be THE anthem for women transitioning back to the world of work.

Today Is Your Day is a solid dose of inspiration with some real-life insight added in for good measure. Shania's voice is better than ever, and the wisdom in her words has legitimate street cred given her journey. It is SOOO worth adding this song to your playlist.

While **Today Is Your Day** is a new favorite, I'll share a couple of other songs that help me get going when I'm losing momentum or just can't seem to kick it in gear.

Unwritten by Natasha Bedingfield: My friend Denise suggested this to me when I was commiserating about writer's block and analysis paralysis. Thanks, Denise!!! I've added it here because for women returning to work after a significant time away, their career future is unwritten and presents a fantastic opportunity to claim their new story, set new goals, and boldly begin their new journey.

Hammer And A Nail by The Indigo Girls: My favorite line — *"The sweetest part is acting after making a decision...."* Yes!!! When women decide to look for their on-ramps back to work, it is indeed sweet to act on their comebacks — researching jobs, polishing skills, writing resumes, and developing their job search strategies.

Firework by Katy Perry: You might adapt these lyrics as a personal mantra — go ahead, show 'em what you ARE worth!! Because returning to work can be scary for women who off-ramped some time ago, confidence often takes a hit. Once they realize their talent, wisdom, life experience and uniqueness, and really understand the value this offers prospective employers, they begin to sparkle! Wonderful!!

This One's For The Girls by Martina McBride: Girl power, country style, big and bold. I defy you to try and NOT sing along.

7 Ideas for Job Search Success

Alas...the season of resolutions is upon us!

The dawn of the new year is a great time to take stock...and to check in and re-calibrate your job search. Below are 7 ideas for you to consider as you begin to look for a job or work to move your search to the next level:

1. **Step away from the computer.** It's very easy to get caught in a cycle of applying to online job postings as your sole job search strategy. Is it possible to find a job this way? Yes. BUT — you significantly increase your chance of job search success by developing a comprehensive strategy that includes other techniques, too. Screen time is not a substitute for face time. Add in appointments and networking events along with a few other techniques and see how your search heats up.

2. **Zero in on your personal brand.** Personal branding is a very hot topic — for good reason. Determining who you are, what you bring to the table and what sets you apart from other job seekers is well worth your time and effort. Your resume will be stronger, your interviews more focused and polished and your brand will carry over into career success.

3. **Leverage social media.** Are you using LinkedIn, Twitter and Facebook to their full job searching potential? The statistics are very clear — social media can help you in your job search. On the flip side, it can also have a negative impact. Be sure your profiles are polished and professional and that any questionable photos and posts are DELETED!!

4. **Join professional organizations and associations.** There is networking gold out there just waiting for you!! Since you won't be spending so much time in front of your computer (remember #1), you'll have time to attend local networking events, alumni gatherings and professional association seminars. Have a supply of business cards and be ready to share your brand through a powerful 'elevator pitch.'

5. **Ask for help.** Resume writing, interviewing, job search strategy development...they are not what they used to be. If you're using the same techniques from years ago, time's a wastin'...and time IS money. Get help. Hire a career coach and/or resume writer who will help you by creating a powerful resume loaded with keywords that will market your skills and successes. He or she can also help you to develop a super job search strategy as well as prepare you to ace interviews. For details on working with a career coach/resume writer, email me.

6. **Go the extra mile whenever you can.** Follow up after networking events, send thank you notes, make phone calls, prepare for interviews, ask questions... there are so many opportunities to distinguish yourself as a job seeker. It's surprising, though, how many candidates don't take advantage of these. You, however, will be sure to do so from now on!

7. **Remember that you are someone's solution.** Yes, it's true. There is a recruiter, HR staffer, manager or coordinator who needs you on his/her team. Your job is to make yourself easy to find. By incorporating some of the ideas listed above, you will be on your way!

ON-RAMPING BOOK SHELF
RECOMMENDATIONS

Recommended Reading

Categories   i = inspiration
                js = job search
                pd = personal development
                r = reinvention

The Age of Miracles — Embracing The New Midlife
by Marianne Williamson (Hay House, 2008) (i, r, pd)

The Art of Extreme Self-Care: Transform Your Life One Month at a Time
by Cheryl Richardson (Hay House, 2009) (i, pd)

The Big Leap — Conquer Your Hidden Fear and Take Life to the Next Level
by Gay Hendricks, Ph.D. (HarperOne, an imprint of Harper Collins, 2009) (I, js, pd, r)

Career Comeback — Repackage Yourself to Get the Job You Want
by Lisa Johnson Mandell (Springboard Press, 2010) (js, pd)

The Desire Map — A Guide to Creating Goals With Soul
by Danielle LaPorte (Sounds True, 2014) (i, pd, r)

Eat That Frog
by Brian Tracy (Berrett Koehler Publishers, 2007) (js, pd)

Expert Resumes for People Returning to Work
by Wendy S. Enelow and Louise M. Kursmark (Jist Works, 2003) (js)

Going Back to Work — A Survival Guide for Comeback Moms
by Mary W. Quigley and Loretta E. Kaufman (St. Martin's Griffin, 2004) (js)

The Job-Hunter's Survival Guide
by Richard N. Bolles (Ten Speed Press, 2009) (js)

The Job Interview Phrase Book
by Nancy Schuman (F & W Media, Inc., 2009) (js)

Job Search Magic — Insider Secrets from America's Career and Life Coach
by Susan Britton Whitcomb (Jist Works, 2006) (js, i, pd)

Knock 'em Dead — The Ultimate Job Search Guide 2011
by Martin Yate, CPC (Adams Media, 2010) (js)

Over 40 & You're Hired
by Robin Ryan (Penguin Books, 2009) (i, js)

The Pathfinder— How to Choose or Change Your Career for a Lifetime of Satisfaction and Success
by Nicholas Lore (Touchstone – a division of Simon & Schuster, Inc., 2011) (I, js, r, pd)

Refuse to Choose
by Barbara Sher (Rodale, 2006) (i, r, pd)

Resume Magic — Trade Secrets of a Professional Resume Writer
by Susan Britton Whitcomb (Jist Works, 2010) (js)

This Is Not the Life I Ordered
by Deborah Collins Stephens, Jackie Speier, Jan Yanehiro and Michealene Cristini Risley (Conari Press, 2007) (i, pd)

What Color Is Your Parachute? 2014: A Practical Manual for Job-Hunters and Career-Changers
by Richard N. Bolles (Ten Speed Press, 2013) (i, pd, js, r)

What You're Really Meant To Do
by Robert Steven Kaplan (Harvard Business Review Press, 2013) (pd, js, r)

Wide Open — On Living with Passion and Purpose
by Dawna Markova, Ph.D. (Conart Press, 2008) (i)

The 6 Reasons You'll Get the Job: What Employers Look For — Whether They Know It Or Not
by Debra Angel MacDougall and Elisabeth Harney Sanders-Park (Prentice Hall Press, 2010) (js, pd)

50 Is the New Fifty
by Suzanne Braun Levine (Penguin Group, 2009) (i, r)

301 Smart Answers to Tough Interview Questions
by Vicky Oliver (Sourcebooks, Inc., 2005) (js)

HELPFUL WEBSITES
FOR ON-RAMPERS

Helpful Wesites for Women Returning to Work

Job Search/Career Websites And Blogs

Brazen Careerist (www.brazencareerist.com)
Entrepreneur and start-up whiz Penelope Trunk's information packed blog. While it's written for the GenY crowd, good information (that's pretty much everything here) is ageless.

Forbes – Career section (www.forbes.com/careers)
Chock full of topics, strategies and insights for job seekers, the regular columnists have their fingers on the pulse of hiring, career paths and career success.

Jobs and Moms.com (http://jobsandmoms.typepad.com/jobs_and_moms/)
Career coach and author Nancy Collamer's site has information tailored to women returning to work.

Job Seekers – Looking For The On Ramp (www.lookingfortheonramp.com)
my professional website.

Wall Street Journal – Career pages (http://online.wsj.com/public/page/news−career−jobs.html)
Well-researched articles on careers, trends, opportunities, and work−life balance for job seekers at all levels and ages.

Training Sites

Community Based Adult Schools/Community Colleges
The prospect of learning new skills or updating current ones can be intimidating, expensive, time consuming, just plain hard…those are a few common refrains. The fact is that without updated and/or relevant skills in a job seekers targeted area, the chance of landing a job shrinks dramatically. So… check out courses and programs (often low cost) offered through your local adult school or community college.

Ed2Go (http://www.ed2go.com)
Online/virtual classes on an amazingly wide array of topics related to both career and self-development. From business to healthcare, personal development, computers, and creative fields — there really does seem to be something here for everyone. Courses range in length and price (though the value and affordability of even the more expensive programs is exceptional).

Formal Online Degree and Certificate Programs at universities around the country can provide desired (and sometimes necessary) credentials. These sometimes come at a savings compared to traditional, on-site courses of study. Google your field of study for possibilities. Note: the technology can vary from recorded sessions with no/little feedback to online meeting rooms where you're working on projects, giving and receiving feedback and required, graded assignments. Personally, I'm partial to the programs with more rigor as it's all about the 'ROI' — return on investment. The more that is required of me (and provided by the instructor), the greater the benefit!

Lynda.com (www.lynda.com) is an online computer training and tutorial site that address entry level to advanced technical skills. For a small monthly fee, subscribers can select video tutorials on a continually developing list of creative, business and technical software to update and add skills that can impact employment marketability and opportunity.

Massive Open Online Courses

MOOCs (http://www.mooc—list.com) lists hundreds, possibly thousands, of free online courses on subjects ranging from Aboriginal art to zoology taught by faculty at some of the country's most prestigious universities. Foreign languages, literature, music, computer software, science…the depth of the offerings is astounding. If you're considering a new career path, this might be a low-risk way to test the waters. If you need to update or brush up on skills in an area where you already have a good foundation, this could be your solution.

Quistic (www.quistic.com)

Brazen Careerist's Penelope Trunk's newest business idea launch. For a fee, it offers online courses on work—related topics such as freelancing, salary negotiation, and Myers Briggs personality types and careers, Quistic can be a very worthwhile stop for job seekers still in exploration mode.

Topic/Skill Specific Training

It is mind boggling to consider the online resources for enhancing and developing skills! Perform a search of the skill you're interested in adding to your skill set as a way to begin your research. Of course, perform full due diligence prior to sharing any personal information and payment. If something seems too good to be true, it most likely is. Look for affiliations with well-established organizations and schools, read reviews and endorsements, and google the company name. Look up key people using LinkedIn or an online search engine. Again, as it bears repeating, do plenty of research BEFORE sharing personal information or making payment. There are many reputable companies out there…sadly, however, there are also people and organizations that are very questionable and are promoting nothing more than scams.

Social Media Sites

Yes, social media is here to stay. It is most certainly not a fad. Nor is it something 'just for kids.' Anyone interested in receiving a paycheck needs to be aware of the power of social media and networking.

LinkedIn is a professional networking site that is used as a kind of 'who's who' directory. Human resources staff may use it as a way to learn more about a prospective applicant. Recruiters are using it to search for qualified candidates, too. LinkedIn also has a searchable careers tab that sorts by location and years of experience. If you're not on LinkedIn, check out the site's learning library for some ideas for getting started. Free accounts provide many benefits that will most likely fit your needs.

Some additional sites to consider are Facebook, Pinterest, Twitter and Google+. Each site has its pluses and minuses as well as slightly different purposes and best practices.

Job Boards

Using job boards to search for opportunities can be a useful part of a job search strategy. However, using online job boards only does not a strategic job search make. Networking, researching, learning…and more are also essential parts of the equation.

Niche job boards — those dedicated to a particular field or job function – are great to visit. Find these for your industry by reading professional journals, checking with professional associations, asking friends and colleagues and even conducting an online search ("job boards for _____").

Some of the big players on the job board scene are Indeed.com, Careerbuilder.com, and Monster.com.

END NOTES

[1] 'at home'...show me a woman who stays 'at home' and I'll show you my barn filled with live, glitter-eating unicorns! In other words, 'stay at home moms' are mythical as women who off-ramp don't really stay at home. They're out and about, meeting, connecting, supervising, managing, sharing, doing and accomplishing! Note: I don't subscribe to the so-called 'mommy wars' that pits moms who work outside the home against those who don't collect a paycheck. The decision for which path to take is highly personal and dependent upon many factors. I prefer the viewpoint that there is room for us all in this big, beautiful stockpot of cities, towns and communities across the land! When I've gathered women together, we often marvel at how we can gaze enviously at some pieces of the different choice made by one group while also appreciating some of the perks of our own choice. Anecdotally, my friends – both paycheck-collecting and not — appreciate the challenges and tribulations of both sides of the issue.

[2] sacred is often thought of as a religious term. In this context, I'm referring to the definition as 'highly valued and important' and 'entitled to reverence and respect' as described in Merriam Webster online (http://www.merriam—webster.com/dictionary/sacred).

[3] job clubs: gatherings of job seekers focused on strategies for successful job searching. The job clubs I lead include time spent on clarifying goals, creating a customized, strategic job search action plan, creating powerful career marketing documents, understanding and communicating each person's unique value proposition, and general supportive brainstorming around careers and success.

[4] support can be in the form of simply reaching out to friends and family, joining in groups designed to provide space and place for sharing concerns, or connecting with a mental health professional or trusted clergy for counseling. If you're feeling overwhelmed, check with your community hospital, physician or local resource hotline for information on what is available near you.

[5] Louise Hay, *You Can Heal Your Life*, 1999, Hay House, Inc., Carlsbad, CA.

[6] Louise Hay, *Love Yourself, Heal Your Life Workbook*, 1990, Hay House, Inc., Carlsbad, CA.

[7] Ruth Kraus, *The Carrot Seed*, 2004, Harper Collins.

[8] This email offer may be withdrawn by the author at any time. Sharing or reproducing the material is strictly prohibited.

Quotes from *You Can Heal Your Life and Love Yourself, Heal Your Life Workbook* are used thanks to the generous permission of Hay House, Inc.

Acknowledgments

Writing a book is a daunting prospect. After the seed of an idea takes hold and germinates, it takes much water, sun and tending to yield the bloom.

I am grateful to my dear friends who cheered me on and provided continual encouragement long beyond any reasonable timeline. Sending this manuscript off was not all that unlike putting my children on the kindergarten bus for the first time. And the group to whom I am grateful could easily be called 'Carol's Book Doulas' for their contributions by way of love, insight, friendship and laughter helped me to birth these pages.

Thank you, thank you, thank you for your support, cheerleading, love and laughter...Jim Camerino, Robby Camerino, Jayne Camerino, Barbara Gromwaldt, Carol Passaro, Nancy Harth, Julianne Edge, Kelly Edge, Judy & John Galiney, Karen & Rich Kuhrt, Katie & Kevin Michels, Eileen & Tom Francavilla, Lynne & Mike Vellucci, Tom & Lisa DeMuro, Richard & Joanna Terry, Ian & Heather Greg, Janet Cargill, Kathy Kane, Denise Williams, Maria Semple and Lynel DeRose.

Additional thanks to Pat Pickard (Pat Pickard Design, www.patpickard.com) for her stunning design aesthetic on the cover and layout of **Words for the Journey**. I still marvel at the serendipity that brought us together to work the refreshment table at our daughters' high school basketball game. I actually showed up for the wrong shift...but realize now the timing was perfect!

About Carol Camerino
CCM, CCMC, CTTCC, CBBSC

Carol Camerino is a back to work strategist, career coach and resume writer dedicated to helping job seekers find their on-ramps to work and career. From new grads seeking their first professional opportunity to parents returning to work after a significant time away, career changers and job seekers looking for career advancement, Carol is passionate about helping them through coaching, strategizing and creating powerful career marketing materials. In addition, she leads workshops, facilitates job clubs and delivers presentations to empower job seekers and support their career success.

Carol's approach to working with clients comes from a genuine desire to be of service. Her clients remark about her compassion, knowledge, encouragement and ability to inspire them to action as well as her skill in transforming resumes and cover letters from bland to compelling while helping them to clarify their skills, achievements and value propositions for prospective employers.

She is a Certified Career Management Coach (CCMC), a Certified Tough Transitions Career Coach (CTTCC), a Certified Brain Based Success Coach (CBBSC) and a Credentialed Career Master (CCM) as well as an associate with the Career Thought Leaders Consortium and a member of the National Resume Writers' Association.

Carol regularly presents at meetings and conferences in addition to working with private clients and leading workshops and seminars.

To discuss having Carol present at your next meeting or conference, email her at Carol@LookingForTheOnRamp.com.

To learn more about Carol, visit Carol's website (www.lookingfortheonramp.com) and blog (www.lookingfortheonramp.blogspot.com)

To receive Carol's enewsletter, email her at Carol@LookingForTheOnRamp.com and ask to be added to her distribution list.

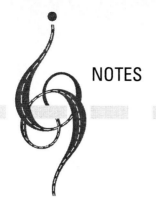

NOTES

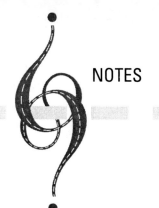

NOTES

NOTES

NOTES